BE THE MANATEE

Affirming Advice for Your Leadership Journey

Dr. Sarah T. Lukas and Dr. Carla L. Sparks

Foreword by Dr. Daniel C. Buckman

Illustrated by Katie L. Sparks Jones

Published by Two Penny Publishing
850 E Lime Street #266
Tarpon Springs, FL 34688
TwoPennyPublishing.com
info@twopennypublishing.com

For permission requests and ordering information, email the publisher at:
info@twopennypublishing.com

ISBN: 978-1-950995-76-9
eBook also available

Library of Congress Control Number: 2022915481

FIRST EDITION

For more information about the authors or to book them for your next event or media interview, please contact their representative at: info@twopennypublishing.com

Two Penny Publishing is a partnership publisher of a variety of genres. We help first-time and seasoned authors share their stories, passion, knowledge, and experiences that help others grow and learn. Please visit our website: TwoPennyPublishing.com if you would like us to consider your manuscript or book idea for publishing.

Endorsements

When I read *Be the Manatee*, I felt like the authors were speaking directly to me in every chapter. They addressed situations that I and most other school leaders have encountered, but with wise and practical answers. If leaders have not experienced some of these challenges, they certainly will at some point in time during their careers. It was an enjoyable and thought-provoking read.

Dr. Bradley Fuller
Elementary School Principal, and current Adjunct Professor of Educational Leadership

This is such an inspirational book, and as I read it, I had a hard time putting it down. This book is so vital to new leaders in the profession of educational leadership and beyond. The analogies Sarah and Carla have so skillfully crafted can be helpful to many individuals who are walking this journey called leadership! The teachable moments from the stories are priceless. I strongly recommend this book as part of any organization's professional development program, aspiring leaders program, or preparing new principals program to make sure new leaders have the tools in their "wheelhouse" to be successful. The book will teach inexperienced and experienced leaders how to navigate the waters to avoid the sharks and any other harmful predator as they take this leadership stroll!

Dr. Rosita Riley
Retired Area Superintendent and School Principal, and current Professional Adjunct Lecturer of Educational Leadership

Using a unique storytelling style, the authors of *Be the Manatee* take both new and experienced leaders on a thought-provoking journey through the different metaphorical animals they may encounter during their leadership journey. A great book for a personal read or a group book study!

Dr. Lorrie Butler

Retired Elementary School Principal, and current Adjunct Professor of Educational Leadership

Dr. Sparks and Dr. Lukas share their diverse perspectives of leadership issues that transcend specific types of workplaces. Describing unique qualities of animals, they creatively develop recommendations for navigating complex human leadership situations. This book is engaging, easy to read, and I recommend it for aspiring, new, or experienced leaders at any level of an organization.

Dr. Stefanie Cedar Shames

Retired School District Administrator and School Principal, and current Adjunct Professor of Educational Leadership

We dedicate this book to leaders, formal and informal, who do the hard work of removing barriers, guiding people through change, and continuing to serve even when things get tough.

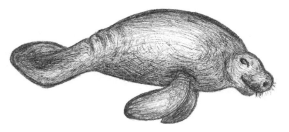

The Manatee
Page 21

The Groundhog
Page 33

The Bat
Page 45

The Butterfly
Page 57

The Bowerbird
Page 71

The Capybara
Page 83

Table of Contents

Part III Avoiding Toxic Behavior

Foreword

I spent my entire public school career pursuing my passion for teaching and leading as a teacher and administrator. Immediately after graduating from college, I obtained a teaching position at a high school. After teaching for 10 years, I became a school-based administrator, first as an assistant principal, then as a principal in three high schools. Continuing my passion for education, I landed a district-level Associate Superintendency for the school district. After spending 30 years in public education, I retired. Not ready to sit in a rocking chair, I knew I still had more to offer to the world of education. I decided to move into higher education by obtaining a full-time faculty teaching position with National Louis University (NLU), where I served as the Chair of the Education Programs in Florida and, more specifically, taught in the Educational Leadership Division for NLU.

During my 12-year tenure with National Louis University, I had the pleasure of meeting the authors of this book, *Be the Manatee*. Dr. Carla Sparks and Dr. Sarah Lukas were doctoral candidates at NLU, and I had the pleasure of facilitating portions of their educational journey. What's intriguing in their collaboration is the 30-year age span between them. Even more fascinating is the breadth and depth of their leadership knowledge, from a very seasoned and successful public school education career with Dr. Sparks to one that's just beginning and building with Dr. Lukas.

These two professionals' collective years of experience, which is the foundation of their book, is remarkable. It's one of those books that you won't be able to put down after you take the initial plunge. The authors take turns providing real-life leadership experiences in a narrative format and then the peer author offers a brief reflective commentary. After the commentary, you find a place to journal prompted by a series of questions that spark reflective thinking. In a unique way of organizing their leadership experience narratives, you will also have the privilege of seeing a living creature take center stage, providing a visual that helps you relate to their story. For example, you will experience leadership lessons through the qualities of a groundhog, bat, butterfly, wolf, mosquito, and shark, just to mention a few. I never thought of using a living creature before when telling a story about leadership, but now I am a believer.

This book reminds me of a leadership experience I faced back in my public school days. My visual metaphor for my story is the flightless bird known as an ostrich. According to the ancient Romans, as we all know, an ostrich tends to "stick its head in the sand." Now we all know that's not true; however, I still like playing off that metaphor as I reflect on my leadership journey. There is absolutely no way that I would ever stick my head in the sand to avoid a tough decision or any other difficulty that I might have faced during my career. If I ever were to do so, I could have hurt my students, faculty, and surrounding community. It was my intent never to let that happen. Case in point, in my first year as a high school principal, I worked hard with the faculty and the surrounding community to generate a culture that all could be proud of, with RESPECT being center stage and what was needed as the focal point at the time. At the close of my inaugural year, there was a school shooting during the summer. Another element noteworthy to mention, I happened to be on my first family vacation after taking on the principalship. I was so blessed that nobody died in that shooting and that my administrative team at the school kicked in gear and immediately started triaging the situation. The very thing great administrative teams discuss and practice for, but hope will never come to fruition, had happened. Upon my immediate return to the school, I could have "stuck my head in the sand" and just carried on letting the experience pass on its own. However, that would have ruined all that we accomplished in our first year. Instead, much work needed to be completed so as to maintain the pride of the school, the dignity of the students, and the reputation of the high school moving forward. We did not have a mass exodus of students because they knew that this was an anomaly and we had it under control. In other words, we cared about them and would work even harder to protect them as if they were our own family.

So you say to yourself, why should I read this particular book? See if this resonates with you. When teaching future leaders how to become the best they can be at their craft, I always shared with them three things they needed for success. First, to be well-read. Get into the periodicals, the excellent textbooks focusing on leadership and study outstanding leaders. Secondly, surround yourself with other professionals who will work hard for the organization's greater good. You don't want people to think like you; you want people to work together and challenge each other to be the best they can be. Thirdly, and I would say most importantly, read case studies that are examples of what other leaders have faced during their careers.

There's nothing better than being transported to an experience of another individual while reading their case study, which focuses on a particular difficulty they experienced and what they did to manage it and keep it in check. It's nice to be a "backseat quarterback," reading about their experience and then having the opportunity to see the outcome. Somebody else's experience will help you if you face a similar situation. In other words, metaphorically speaking, you're putting extra arrows in your quiver. I always liked to have a quiver packed with experiences that I could pull from if ever needed. It made me a better leader, well-rounded if you will. So, I challenge you to pick up this book written by two very professional leaders and add it to your repertoire of resources. You won't be disappointed, I promise you.

Daniel C. Buckman, Ed.D.

A Note from the Authors

We are so glad you are here. Chances are, if you are reading this book, you are interested in a leadership position in your field or are currently serving in a leadership capacity within your organization—congratulations! This book is an opportunity to read about various true-life experiences we have had over the years in our leadership positions and the actions and mindsets that helped us persevere and succeed. We want to help you process and prosper while you transition or progress in your position.

An interesting note about us as we share our various stories with you: while kindred in spirit, we are thirty years apart in age. This generational gap allows us to provide you with different perspectives on leadership issues, though you may find after reading our stories that we share the same leadership values.

The two of us really hit it off through the dissertation writing process. Carla was the chair, or lead professor, of Sarah's dissertation and worked closely with her as she completed her research. We found that our weekly conversations on the progress of Sarah's dissertation quickly turned into an hour (if not two) of discussing our daily lives at work and at home. We related to each other on a deep level as both of us were going through a transition at the time. In the spring of 2018, Carla had recently retired from a leadership position in a large, public K-12 school district and joined the faculty of National Louis University full-time. Sarah was finishing up her first year as a public school district administrator, made particularly difficult as it was a new position, and she was new to the district. Our conversations became a time to process and problem-solve through difficult moments. Our friendship grew, and we learned a lot from each other during those weekly conversations.

So, what does it mean to *be the manatee*? As you will read more in Chapter 1, the answer lies in a difficult season for Sarah. While at her desk, processing a particularly tough moment, a trait about one of her favorite animals, the Florida manatee, surfaced in her mind. She realized if she could metaphorically take on this trait, she could overcome the mental barriers built during the present difficulty. We talked about that moment and found that the traits of the manatee could be applied in numerous leadership scenarios. The phrase *be the manatee* became a metaphor of encouragement whenever one of us needed to hear it.

Through our subsequent weekly conversations, we found that animals continued to come up when discussing points in our respective leadership journeys. These metaphors allowed us to gain perspective, find positivity, and grow, while the connection to animals helped embed these lessons in our memories. We hope that through these animal metaphors and stories, you build a toolbox of mindsets to access as you continue your leadership journey.

An Important Note

Not every experience we will share with you is positive. We have seen examples of what not to do as a leader. However, each of these experiences taught us a great deal. You can absolutely learn from non-examples (sometimes we were our own non-examples!). When we share these stories, it is not intended to be unkind. Anonymity is maintained because the goal of these examples is to share a difficult moment for us in our own journeys and the leadership lessons gained. We have no ill will towards any leaders in these stories and appreciate the lessons—even if it was tough at the time.

How to Use This Book

You will notice that we do not have chapter numbers. That is on purpose! This book is meant to lift you up when you find you need some advice on your leadership journey. Feel free to read the question that accompanies each chapter in the table of contents as a guide to decide what you need most in the moment.

Some chapters are written from Sarah's experience, while others are written by Carla. You will find that each of us writes a response to each other in which we share a relevant story to the chapter topic. This approach allows you to read about a variety of scenarios in which you may find yourself. Plus, as we mentioned above, we are thirty years apart in age and experience—regardless of where you are in your leadership journey, this book has something to offer you.

Each chapter concludes with reflection questions and some space to take some notes, make a journal entry, or jot down next steps. We encourage you to take advantage of that space because you likely read the chapter because you needed it. What better time to plan how to move forward and get you out of the tough spot in which you may have found yourself?

We hope that reading these stories provides as much comfort and encouragement as we experienced when we told them to each other. Enjoy!

PART I

Protecting
Your Peace

*Simply put, sharks are not
a factor for manatees.*

THE MANATEE

*What if I feel surrounded by people
who want to hurt me or my career?*

My mind becomes very creative when under stress. Perhaps my inner self is trying to make sense of the anxiety and worry zooming around my brain, or perhaps my brain is just firing on all cylinders, and creativity is the byproduct of all that nervous and productive energy. Either way, the idea for this book and the metaphor that started it all was a result of enduring such high stress that I experienced physical pain. I clearly remember sitting at my desk, my hands aching from my current physical manifestation of stress, and for some reason, animal facts started floating to the surface of my mind...

That day at my desk was particularly difficult. I served in a leadership role within my organization, and my senior leaders had recently tasked me with launching an initiative. In order to pull it off, I had to handle a lot of different elements at once. There was the substance of the initiative, which was truly the easy part as I dedicated a lot of time to reading, researching, and observing other organizations where this initiative was already successful. My brain could handle that. It was the external factors that kept me awake at night, my stomach in knots, and my hands aching–factors like budget, stakeholder buy-in, and nay-sayers. It was a very public initiative, and eyes were on me.

Frankly, my job may have been on the line if the whole thing didn't go well. The pressure was incredible. On this difficult day, criticism had come my way from an important person within my organization, and it was not constructive. It did not come from a place of concern or assistance. It was just personal criticism loosely connected to my project efforts that about caused me to break down—but then my brain had a little spark of an idea that helped me move past that terribly difficult moment. At that moment, I had an epiphany.

To provide some context, I grew up in central Florida. Here, teachers taught how to escape an alligator and avoid a shark attack alongside long division and the scientific method. So on that particularly challenging day, molded by my Florida experience, I felt surrounded by proverbial sharks of undue stress and criticism. When the epiphany struck, I remembered a fact about manatees that almost instantly made me feel better. Manatees, the large, serene, aquatic mammals, have no natural predators—not even sharks. This fact helped me shift my mindset and move forward.

In Florida waters, sharks are powerful predators in the local ecosystem, and yet, manatees rarely become their prey when migrating through the Gulf of Mexico or the Atlantic Ocean. Manatees are protected by their behavior as they do not swim in the same area as sharks.[1] Simply put, sharks are not a factor for manatees. As leaders, sharks may take any number of forms. One may be a superior lacking empathy. Another may be colleagues who lack growth mindsets or the will to collaborate. Sharks could be customers, parents of students at the school you lead, or clients who never seem to be pleased.

I stopped internalizing my stress by internalizing the idea of "being the manatee" in waters seemingly full of sharks waiting to prey on others. Sharks may exist, but I did not have to swim in their waters and be susceptible to their behavior. My worth was not my work. I was capable, and I gave myself permission to learn and grow. Since that period of my leadership journey, I have continued to serve in leadership positions, and inevitably, a shark has entered the scenario. But by developing a "manatee mentality," I learned to avoid feeling attacked or becoming a shark myself.

For the sake of transparency (and reality), mentally aligning myself with the characteristics of the manatee was helpful *in that moment*. I remember feeling a sense of relief as the thought pulled me out of my stress spiral and reminded me that the world is bigger than this one initiative and I would be okay. It really helped. But I did have to keep reminding myself to *be the manatee* when times got tough and actively work through difficult times by focusing my productivity on finishing a stressful task, seeking help to improve my mental health, and surrounding myself with people who supported me and my efforts.

The manatee also provided another lesson. They swim to warmer waters and gather together in order to survive when the water they are currently swimming in becomes too cold (see Footnote 1). While working through this new and difficult initiative for my organization, I developed additional professional and personal relationships with people vital to my success. These people knew more about the initiative's substance, helped me best spend the budget, and helped me cultivate the buy-in I needed, connecting me with important stakeholders. When I was around them, the waters were much warmer!

Furthermore, I could rely on my colleagues who may not have been directly involved in the project but understood that it was big and supported my efforts. My friends, family, and mentors outside of the organization were also critical in reminding me that I had no sharks to worry about and to keep floating along. That one idea, that one reminder of an animal fact I learned somewhere in my time as a young student in Florida, truly moved me forward.

In the end, the initiative met the original goals set by my senior leaders. The project continued for multiple years, and therefore, I considered it a success. I also considered it a success even more so because I lived through it. I learned from it, I gained experience, and I still value the relationships that stemmed from that time.

There is a strong possibility that some point in your leadership journey will be difficult. A task may be out of your area of expertise, and the amount you have to learn may be significant. An initiative may, if successful, cause a paradigm shift within your organization and therefore be met with resistance. Or a task may be easy enough, but the amount of criticism you receive may be high, even if you execute it well. Regardless of the scenario, remember to *be the manatee*. Seek warm waters, avoid those who put you down, and you'll swim out on the other side just fine.

Carla's Response

Sarah and I were having one of the many detailed and heartfelt discussions we have had over the years about work, leadership, how to make a difference, how to serve others in meaningful ways, how to lead change, and how difficult it all seems at times. We were both serving in leadership roles in different organizations. At that time, I was a mentor to Sarah, serving as her dissertation committee chairperson, while she was traveling through her doctoral journey. However, during this particular discussion, I was the one who needed encouragement. An important thing to remember about being a leader of important work involving people is that it can be challenging at any age and with any amount of experience. I was dealing with a challenging time.

One of my mentoring techniques is to share a personal experience, past or present, with my mentee who has just shared a frustrating challenge with me. I like to let my mentees know that I, too, feel frustrated at times, and there is always a way through the frustration. During that particular discussion with Sarah, I was not just sharing a personal experience to let her know I could relate to her distress, but I was sharing from my heart about a challenging time through which I was traveling. Suddenly, Sarah said to me, "Be the manatee, Carla." I did not know what she meant at first. Then Sarah shared with me, as she shared with you, that the manatee has no natural predators. Sarah also reminded me that manatees are herbivores. She pointed out that because they are herbivores, manatees do not prey on other animals. Huh.

The concept of an animal who is not preyed upon and does not prey upon others was a startling thought. As I thought about what that might be like, Sarah helped me process the notion and how I could use it to help me think about the problem at hand. I have found that in leadership, dealing with difficult people and challenging situations usually means adjusting my own frame of mind. As Sarah and I continued to talk about what it means to be the manatee and how to translate the concept to work scenarios, I began to experience a mind shift.

For me, thinking of myself as a manatee means that I realize people at work cannot really hurt me. Sometimes people seem cruel, but it is helpful to assume good intentions. Now, I am not naïve, and I realize that sometimes people are intentionally hurtful, but at work, it is helpful to assume good intentions—that is part of being a manatee. When I consider that people are not showing up each day with the intention of doing poor work, making bad decisions, or hurting someone else's feelings, then I am able to look at my leaders and those whom I lead in a more positive light. This mindset helps me see things from their point of view and understand how they feel and why they do and say things. That leads me to not prey on them. It is never my intention as a leader to behave like a predator. I want to lead people to meet their goals and to make the organization strong and successful. I never lie awake at night thinking of ways I can hurt people and put up barriers to their success; however, when I feel hurt, I occasionally lash out in defense, which results in hurting others. While my hurting others is unintentional, the outcome is still *damaging. When I remember to be the manatee, I do not allow others to hurt me, and I do not become defensive and hurt them unintentionally.*

Sarah continues to remind me to be the manatee. She can tell when I am having a bad day. She lets me vent, and then gives me the important reminder to be the manatee. The reminder from Sarah does not change any of the facts in my challenges; however, it does change my frame of thinking, which is what I can truly control. When I am in control of my thoughts, feelings, and ways of viewing people and situations, then I can help others. And I feel better.

Take Time to Reflect

- Think back to a difficult time in your leadership journey. What made it difficult? What was in your control and what was not?

- **Challenge:** When you find yourself with difficulty ahead of you, what can you do to swim to warmer waters as you complete the task and move through the difficult moment?

- **Making Progress:** What do you need? Whose help do you need to get there?

BE THE MANATEE

BE THE MANATEE

I was becoming prepared and refreshed to do work that I deemed important, interesting, and meaningful to educators and their students.

THE GROUNDHOG

What do I do when I start to feel useless?

I once wore a badge that declared me to be a data analyst. That's right. I had been a third-grade teacher, a middle school teacher, a high school English teacher, and a district resource teacher. After years and years of teaching students to write and to write well, I was now a data analyst. I had developed a high school academy of journalism, and I had directed the growth and implementation of that program and the five publications our students created. I had been teaching creative writing, journalistic writing, and digital design. I had been taking students to conferences and competitions, and they were winning. I had been developing curricula and teaching other educators to develop curricula. I worked with people and words for more than two decades, and then I was a data analyst. Numbers!

Just months prior, I was flying around the United States, delivering conference presentations on how to collaborate with school district partners and make school engaging for teachers and students. I had also been attending conference sessions presented by other educators from around the country and gathering ideas from them to improve my own practice and guide my work as a leader. I was traveling locally from school to school and to various community colleges and private post-secondary institutions to inform counselors and school leaders about career options for students. I was forging partnerships and writing articulation agreements to make it possible for high school students to enter college with some of their college credits already earned in high school. I was making a difference, and I could feel it every day.

While I loved the work I was doing, the dynamics were shifting. So, I decided it was time for a change, and I became a number cruncher. I found myself driving downtown to the main school district building that housed the superintendent, the school board, and scores of district administrators. I parked my little red Mustang with the white convertible top in the parking lot, and there it sat for 10-12 hours each day, waiting for me to come out of my semi-dark cubicle and drive it home. During those 10-12 hours, I counted students, I counted schools, and I counted the number of student seats a school could hold. I added up the numbers, I created databases, and I worked in databases other people created. I worked with district administrators and parents to determine special school assignments for students. I learned how to run a lottery for magnet school placements. I fielded phone calls from parents who had questions or demands regarding their children's school assignments. I was a data analyst, and I was happy to be learning new skills related to my new role. I was happy for the change from the frenetic travel in my previous position and to know I was going to the same building every day and developing new professional relationships.

The Value of Hibernating

Eventually, I began to miss the feeling I had before—that feeling of making a difference in someone's life. While there were undoubtedly benefits in my position as a data analyst, I began to feel that I was not making a difference in anyone's life. I wondered what I could do to help anyone while working in a cubicle with spreadsheets and a telephone. I prayed every day that I would make a positive impact on somebody's life, but I could not see or feel that happening. What I did not realize, and what I could not see or possibly know, was that I was a groundhog and hibernating, metaphorically speaking.

Hibernation is a way for animals to save up energy by lowering metabolic functions when temperatures are extreme.[2] There's more to hibernation than you think: hibernating is just one way animals survive the coldest part of the year, but it takes on many different forms. Groundhogs are among the few animals who are considered to be true hibernators. They fatten themselves in warm seasons and then sleep for about three months during the cold season. During hibernation, the groundhog's heart rate slows to about five beats per minute. Their breathing drops to about two breaths per minute.[3] They dig burrows that can be as deep as six feet and up to twenty feet long with multiple entrances. These deep burrows provide a safe place for fat and slow groundhogs to hide from predators, who can run more than twice as fast as they can.

I was exhausted from the constant motion required in my previous role. During my two years as a data analyst, I did not travel around the country. I really did not miss keeping a travel bag ready to hop on a plane and fly to another state, dragging a rolling cart filled with a laptop, flash drive, and training materials. I did not drive from school to school. I did not visit colleges and other post-secondary institutions. My data analyst job was a welcome change at first as I slowed down, worked in my cubicle, and talked to others on the telephone as needed. I was honing some skills and learning new skills using various databases. I was learning a lot of detailed information about the structure of the school district in which I had now been busily working for over twenty years. I now needed to know how many students there were, how many schools there were, and information related to placing the correct number of students in each school to meet state regulations for voter-approved class sizes. Yet, I failed to see the real importance of these details in terms of changing people's lives.

As time marched on, I became a bit bored and more concerned about my lack of positive impact on others. Nevertheless, I continued to work long hours and learn new things. My boss taught me to make pivot tables, prepare reports, and use my digital design skills to develop publications for the school district. I was busy, for sure. But still, the glamour of travel and teaching educators from across the country were no longer part of my work world, and I felt somewhat useless.

Before the two years were over, my boss realized I was the one person on her staff with experience developing curricula. I guess she missed that part of my resume when I applied to work on her district-office staff. She eventually asked me to take on special assignments related to grant-funded programs while continuing my data analyst duties. This groundhog was beginning to wake up. I started venturing out of my cubicle and into my little red Mustang to visit schools again. The schools I visited were implementing a variety of interesting instructional programs. Some of those programs were magnet programs by design, and others were voluntary public school choice programs. It became my responsibility to work with teachers and school administrators to ensure they had the knowledge, skills, and material resources needed to increase student learning through their special programs. As I did so, I slowly began to realize the new skillset I had gained during my hibernation period was vitally important to the curriculum work that had come my way. That hibernation time had been well spent after all. While it seemed I was doing little to help others, in reality, I was becoming prepared and refreshed to do work that I deemed important, interesting, and meaningful to educators and their students. I was becoming realigned for the next phase of my career. My time being a groundhog was a necessary time of learning, refreshing, and realigning in preparation for the next phase of my leadership journey.

Sarah's Response

It was the summer of 2006. I was home from my first year as an undergraduate, and it was time to get a job. One of the first days I was home, I found myself at an office supply retail store with my dad, picking up something, and the manager asked me if I needed a job because they were hiring seasonal employees. Clearly, this was fate, I thought to myself. So, for two and a half months, I sold electronics to the good people of Central Florida.

Like Carla's experience, changing from a teacher focused on writing to a data analyst buried in numbers, I was a music major who traded clarinet reeds for a name tag and warranty plan pamphlets. I was unsure how well my sales technique would develop in a short amount of time, but I have to say, thanks to a great department supervisor and some training, I got pretty good!

I learned how to meet the needs of the customer by listening to what they had to say and then connecting them to the ideal product (You keep running out of ink in your inkjet printer, and you're tired of buying ink refills? Why don't you try a laserjet?). I learned how to talk to customers in a way that opened conversation (don't start with a "yes" or "no" question) to close a sale. I learned to overcome barriers, such as adjusting my approach when customers would rather talk to a man about electronics than a young woman (confidence in your knowledge of the products is key).

By the end of the summer, my sales numbers were the highest on the team, and even though it was only a couple of months, I had a new set of skills under my belt that would not truly reveal their use again until I was teaching students and leading others. In my case, it was not me who hibernated, but the skills. I found a lot of similarities between salesmanship and trying to get a teenager interested in history or a staff person on board with a new initiative. You must listen and determine needs, generate buy-in, and overcome barriers. Years after my time in retail, I still smile to myself occasionally as I move through various teaching and leadership scenarios because, sometimes, the skill set I use to help a colleague or teach others is similar to the skill set I used to sell a printer.

Never take a job, position, or change for granted because you may find yourself gaining experience that will serve you in future roles. Or, as Carla says, you might find yourself in a position to recharge and prepare for an upcoming challenge. Either way, embrace the hibernation, and get excited for what may lie ahead!

Take Time to Reflect

- Have you ever found yourself making a serious or abrupt pivot in your work like I did when I left my work with curriculum and writing to be a data analyst? Describe a time when you took on a task outside your comfort zone and what you took away from that experience.

- Consider a time when you doubted the value of your work. Can you now see how you were being aligned for a new role that became very important? What did you learn during your time of *hibernation*?

- **Challenge:** Think about a time when you had to slow your pace as a leader or in any capacity. How did it go? Consider whether and how you were refreshed and realigned.

- **Making Progress:** What do you need? Whose help do you need to get there?

BE THE MANATEE

BE THE MANATEE

Discernment is
your echolocation.

THE BAT

What if I am surrounded by negativity?

I remember being asked to lead an initiative that involved a lot of change, a lot of funding, and a lot of people. I worked for months to develop my own capacity of knowledge surrounding the initiative, collaborate with necessary partners, build awareness, and then begin to execute the plan. As I transitioned from preparation to actually making changes in the organization, I started to hear things about myself or the initiative from various parts of the organization. Over time, the noise began to pick up. I am not talking about the great advice I received on how best to spend the budget or the requests to work together on trainings. I am talking about the noise with no point aside from being hurtful. The whispers saying, "It won't work," and "I would never," crept into my ears, and then the personal criticism began.

The story above is not unique to me or to one place or to one field. Over time, as I took on leadership roles in different organizations, I quickly noticed that people had a lot to say about my performance and the team I served. Some individuals questioned our qualifications and scrutinized our resumes. Some individuals believed they could perform our roles better. Some commented on my young age or saw my passion for my role as foolish or stubborn. Some were quiet with their comments. Some were not.

At this point, I should note my mind tends to dwell on negative comments for a long time. I hang on to them. It's a problem I am constantly working on; however, I wanted to share that with you because perhaps you can relate to having the desire to excel, going on to achieve excellence, and still mentally clinging to any negative feedback. This mental state can make taking on leadership positions daunting. Therefore, this chapter is even more important to you as taking on any leadership role may result in criticism about your approach or decisions. Because, regardless of how well-thought-out, data-based, or compassion-forward your decisions are, you will never please everyone.

I've been a people pleaser for as long as I can remember. I met criticism with a mix of frustration, anxiety, and sadness every time the noise reached my ears. Sure, I heard more than just constant criticism, but the problem was that when criticism happened, it was louder than the positive feedback. That's how it usually goes, isn't it?

For example, let's return to the personal criticism I experienced as part of the story at the beginning of this chapter. I remember one particular moment when I spoke to a vendor with one of my supervisors, and my supervisor became infuriated at me because my style of active listening (nodding, verbal acknowledgment) was irritating to him. It was a fifteen-minute meeting. One meeting. The criticism was inconsequential in the long run, but wow, does my brain love to hang on to that stuff.

Throughout the course of this massive project and others like it, I've felt as though I wasn't doing enough despite my long hours and meeting my deadlines. The loud criticism drowned out the positive. I have felt like a pariah despite receiving positive feedback on the training sessions I held. I have felt ineffective despite the strong evaluations I received from my supervisor.

Mentally, it was a tough road to navigate, and I can honestly say there were times when I was miserable.

During occurrences of pointless and/or personal negativity, I often found myself at a crossroads. I could sort through the feedback and do something with the helpful pieces, continue to be miserable, refuse to adjust, or leave. While I must be honest and admit there were times I was miserable for a few days or wanted to leave, more often than not, I chose to do something with the feedback and focus my listening through the noise on the things said with sincerity and good intent.

I'm reminded of a misunderstood, nocturnal creature who focuses its hearing on finding sustenance in the darkness—the bat. According to the Maryland Department of Natural Resources, bats utilize the sound they emit to echolocate their food. By focusing their hearing on the sound returning from an object's surface, a bat can adeptly locate a moth, a beetle, or any number of insect snacks even when it's dark outside.[4]

In the case of your role as a leader in your organization, you are the bat. The moth is your vision and goals within the organization, and the darkness is the negative noise through which you are navigating. This metaphor is not meant to suggest that you should only listen to the noise emanating from your own mouth, but rather to focus through what we will call the "nonsense negativity." These are the negative words that are nonsensical in nature (i.e., presumptive due to age, appearance, or even general grumpiness because perhaps the critic wishes that they, or someone they know, were in the job). The words may not be based on reality or anything of substance, but those words can be loud.

It is imperative to your success to focus your hearing on the things you can take as productive feedback and ignore the chatter. This may require a change in your behavior. Perhaps you stop passing by the water cooler. Perhaps you decide that you are going to leave on time each day in order to preserve your mental health. Perhaps you move your desk. Perhaps there are people with whom you decide to spend more or less time. Whatever you need to do to stay focused.

Not everyone may understand, at first, why you changed your behavior, but it is not your job to explain to someone why your mental health is important. A bat can be misunderstood when focusing their hearing on their prey and going after that bug in the sky. Observers often note bats have erratic flight patterns when they are on the hunt. Their catch is more important than following a straight line. While it may seem irrational to observe, this focused hunting is rewarded with moth-y goodness, just as you may be rewarded if you change your patterns to help stay the course (see Footnote 4).

So, how do you define the nonsense negativity from constructive criticism? The key is discernment. Discernment is your echolocation. Consider the source of the information. Is the person providing the commentary on your work someone close enough to the project to see the nuance of the job? Or, do they only know your face and where your nameplate is hung? Determine who you can turn to for help in focusing through the noise. The person who gave you the positive evaluation? Talk to them. The collaborative coworker who is always there to bounce an idea off of and give advice? Talk to them.

This does not mean that negativity and criticism never harbor truth; it just means you may need a trusted colleague or supervisor to help you remember your strengths, plan the next steps, and focus your hearing, so you can catch that moth. That is how the story I shared with you ends. I relied on the people who offered solutions and support to move the initiative forward–the people who understood the goal and the focus it would take to carry it out. They helped me increase my discernment which, in turn, helped me decrease the impact (or volume level) of the nonsense negativity and get the job done.

As I write this, I realize that some of you may not fully understand the people-pleasing, the hanging on to negative words, or the need to focus through the noise because you never struggled with it. You are already a confident little bat who has never missed a moth in your life with your laser-like echolocation skill! I envy you and your ability to get a full night's sleep without being awakened by your own nagging thoughts about what so-and-so said about your latest initiative. Take this chapter, then, as something to keep in your back pocket if the noise ever does reach your ears and causes a distraction. Sometimes, it's not about our personality or brain chemistry that makes us more prone to the noise, but rather how attached we are to a particular project. It's easy to ignore the criticism when your investment in the result is minimal.

The even happier end is that each leadership role I've taken in my career, even if it started with loud, critical noise, truly wound up a positive experience. I had strong relationships with those around me and learned lots of lessons. The noise will decrease as your discernment grows, and it will become easier to surround yourself with supportive people and navigate with competency and compassion (towards yourself especially).

Carla's Response

I can relate to Sarah's personal story about the chatter, the noise, and the distracting and disturbing comments of others. I, too, focus on what other people think and say about me. I can easily fixate on any negative remarks.

During my years as a school district administrator, I planned and conducted many professional development opportunities for teachers. Sometimes, I led the training alone, and sometimes, I worked with a partner or even a small team of instructional leaders. All of these approaches were fun for me. I love interacting with other leaders, and I love interacting with an audience. Simply put, I love teaching.

There are lots of best practices in teaching, and there are additional best practices in teaching adult learners. For example, do something exciting, funny, or dramatic at the beginning of the training session to grab everyone's attention. Make sure to engage the audience throughout the session. Incorporate movement into the teaching and learning. Stimulate accountable talk among the participants. And when you reach the end of the training session, provide the participants an opportunity to give feedback on their experience. Give them a survey or an exit slip. The precise method used is not important, just be sure to get their feedback. Thus begins the noise in my head.

Today, as a college professor, I use these very same best practices to teach leaders how to grow in their own leadership practices. I have found that I use even more instructional strategies now than I did in previous years. I am constantly searching for new ways to help adult learners gather and retain new information to improve their own practices. And I still ask for feedback at the end of each class session. Invariably, I read all the exit slips, surveys, or comment forms before I even leave the room. I am anxious to determine whether I met their needs and if they felt the session was worth their time and tuition.

I have honed my skills over my more than forty years as an educator, so I typically receive positive feedback on sessions I facilitate and presentations I make. However, there is also often at least one "suggestion" for improvement on which I fixate. I know I need to consider using such comments as part of my thinking toward a cycle of improvement, and I do that. Nevertheless, old habits die hard, and I sometimes just fixate on the noise of negativity and start up the old engine of self-doubt. Lucky for me, longevity of experience helps me to put those "suggestions" into perspective and determine whether to a) use them to improve my next class session, b) try to ignore them, or c) wallow in misery and feel like a failure. I choose to feel successful, vibrant, and innovative. I choose to have a growth mindset and constantly work to improve my practice, and I choose to quiet the nonsense negativity.

Take Time to Reflect

- What is your experience with nonsense negativity?

- Is it easy for you to focus through the noise? If so, how do you maintain your healthy mindset? If not, what are the barriers to focusing?

- **Challenge:** The next time you experience noisy, nonsense negativity in connection with your leadership, who can you turn to for help with discernment?

- **Making Progress:** What do you need? Whose help do you need to get there?

_____

_____

_____

_____

_____

_____

_____

_____

_____

_____

_____

_____

BE THE MANATEE

BE THE MANATEE

Apologize when appropriate.
Don't hesitate; just do it.

THE BUTTERFLY

*What if I need to repair the
relationships around me?*

As I worked through various leadership roles throughout my career, I found it essential to hold on to some of the qualities of the butterfly. I found that endurance, as demonstrated by butterflies, was a key ingredient to leading people toward a common goal. I discovered that hope, one of the characteristics some consider to be symbolized by butterflies, was another trait I needed to help me stay the course.

A common saying is that if there is one constant in this life, it is that things will change. The irony of that statement is an important reminder to organizational leaders that change will be part of the leadership role as we consistently work through continuous improvement cycles. The butterfly is an excellent example of enduring change through its metamorphic life. As we know, butterflies begin life as an egg. The caterpillar hatches from that egg and eventually turns into a chrysalis. The final stage of life is when the butterfly emerges as a beautiful, flying creature.

As I look back on my leadership experiences, I recognize the stages of the butterfly's metamorphosis in my work, and I see the importance of enduring change within myself and leading change for others. When I was a butterfly egg, if you will, my work was relatively safe from attack. My superiors gave me directives, and I followed those instructions. That gave me the freedom to be creative while my superiors provided guidance and a safety net. When things became a bit rocky, I told my boss, and she stepped in to stabilize the work. I marched onward. As I became a caterpillar of a leader, it seemed as though few people noticed me, and therefore, I was rarely challenged. Again, at this stage, I felt free, happy to help and make a difference for teachers and students in creative ways. However, my profile became obvious as I matured in my leadership roles and became like the butterfly stretching its wings and taking flight. When a leader holds a high-profile position, naysayers become vocal. Not only are there naysayers among those being led, but other leaders often feel threatened by a fully developed butterfly, so they become naysayers.

Some people are actually afraid of beautiful butterflies. Some are afraid of the fluttering of the butterfly's wings, some people fear a butterfly might land on them, and some are frustrated by the unpredictability of the butterfly's movements. Some butterflies have patterns in their wings that look like the eyes of predators. Some researchers say these eye spots in the wing design that often look like the eyes of an owl, a snake, or even a fox serve to scare away predators by causing them confusion.[5] I found such fear in some people when I stretched my leadership wings. It seems, looking back, that some were intimidated by my abilities and my work ethic. It was as though they felt my butterfly wings threatened to muffle or subdue them, though that was never, ever my intent. My intent was simple—enable students to reach their highest potential, guide teachers to do their best, enjoy the work, and collaborate with other leaders to strengthen the organization. Regardless of the inevitable struggles of leadership, I remained steadfast and strong, like the monarch butterfly.

Perhaps one of the most important lessons in my metamorphosis as a leader was when I realized I was unintentionally frustrating my boss. For a while, I could not understand why she seemed disinterested in my work. She did not have time to discuss the initiatives I was leading. Her demeanor was cold. Then, through a conversation with another leader about some of the difficulties students were having with authority figures, I realized that, like the students who were out of control, my butterfly wings were out of control. My wings had a pattern that caused my boss to see me as a scarier animal than I intended. I needed to continue being a change leader, but I also needed to humble myself and demonstrate that my wings were not a threat but rather a symbol of my desire to be helpful to others. My boss had acquired me as her employee through an internal reorganization; she had not chosen to hire me. I had thought it terribly important to teach her all about the initiatives for which I was responsible, thus to her, flapping my wings in a frustrating way. It finally occurred to me that in the department where I was working, I was the only person whom my boss had not hired. Basically, she was stuck with me.

The fact that my new boss might need some support and assistance from me had escaped me. I was just too busy flapping my wings. I thought about this carefully and then approached my boss with an apology. I walked toward her office, and she appeared disappointed to see me coming. She began to verbalize an assumption about why I was there and what I wanted from her. I quickly opened my mouth and said, "No, I am here to apologize to you." Her eyes widened, her expression changed immediately, and she stepped aside to let me enter her office. Then I told her how sorry I felt when I realized that my wings had gotten too big and looked scarier than they really were and that I had only demonstrated care for the work I was leading and not the bigger picture of the work she was leading. My intention in offering this apology was sincere and with no expectations. Little did I know, my boss was under tremendous work stress at that very moment, and after I humbled myself, she told me about what she was dealing with. She expressed her appreciation to me for coming forward with my apology. She even indicated she thought I was standing in her office doorway because I, again, wanted something from her.

In that conversation, I remember she said to me, "Carla, you just don't know how much this means to me, especially today." She was about to face the school board of a very large public school district, where she would defend an important initiative that was under scrutiny, and I had been oblivious to the fact that the meeting was about to occur. I had been too busy focusing on my goals and initiatives to notice. But from that day forward, we had an open and trusting work relationship. Like the butterfly, I had changed and endured change; I gripped hope, life, and rebirth; and I found a way to spread my wings without causing fear in others.

I learned several lessons that day. The first lesson I took away from that relationship-changing conversation was to not be reluctant to apologize. Some people see the act of apologizing as a sign of weakness. I see it as an opportunity to be sincere, acknowledge mistakes or misjudgments, and consider the feelings of others before my own, even when my feelings are hurt. That last part was critical for me to learn. As a sensitive person, my feelings are easily hurt. But after that single day, that single conversation, when I approached my boss with an apology and she opened up to me, I abruptly learned to consider whether my actions were causing negative reactions in others. I learned to not wallow in my own feelings of hurt and disappointment but rather to think about what I might be doing to cause those hurtful actions done by other leaders. That is a lesson I have not forgotten. Apologize when appropriate. Don't hesitate; just do it.

Another takeaway from that conversation with my boss was to consider the bigger picture. When I am working hard to ensure that the initiatives for which I am responsible develop fruitfully and sustainably, I sometimes do not receive all the support I think I need to get the job done. However, now I stop to think about why I am being told *no* or to wait for funding, staff, materials, or support in general. I think about what is going on in the entire organization.

I think about what restraints my boss is under. I remember that everyone with whom I work wants to help people. We are all in the people business, and as such, receiving a *no* or a *wait* answer to my requests is not because my boss and others do not care. I now realize there are many moving parts in leading an organization, and sometimes, I have to slow down and wait for other parts of the machine to get their work done, so I can move forward. Sometimes, I just have to accept *no* or *wait* for an answer.

The third thing I learned that day was to keep my head up and look around. It is impossible to consider the bigger picture if you are inwardly focused and single-minded about your own work all the time. It is important to remain focused to accomplish goals, and it is also important to pause and look around to be cognizant of what other leaders are doing and *how* they are doing. It is important to gain a sense of when to offer help, or simply moral support, to another leader who needs it.

Apologize, consider the bigger picture, and pay attention to what is going on. As a fully mature butterfly, who busily flaps her wings, I must remember these three lessons. They have helped me to be a better contributor to the overall organization. Being a leader is more than being in charge. It is the willingness to help others.

Sarah's Response

While Carla found herself in a situation where she transitioned between departments inside her organization, you may find when you transition to your next leadership role that it is not within your current organization. You may find yourself in a brand new leadership role as well as a brand new place with brand new people! That very scenario happened to me, and Carla's connection to the butterfly reminds me of that time in my leadership journey.

When I arrived at my new place of work to perform my new role in a new city, I remember being worried about a lot of things all at once. I did not feel like I had the luxury of metamorphosis and growth; rather, I had to show up and know what I was doing from the get-go. I had to flap my butterfly wings confidently and immediately. I stood up for my projects in meetings, I did a lot of research on unfamiliar topics on my own time instead of asking questions, and I did my best to know what I was talking about at all times. No caterpillar stage, no cocoon, no chrysalis.

I got to know people in my organization slowly but surely, and they got to know me. I made friends; I got things done. Butterflies are not often feared once they are seen close-up—little bodies, frail antennae, fragile wings. Who could be intimidated, annoyed, or worried about me? I discovered later, however, that the pattern on my proverbial wings must have looked like something some people did not like, as not everyone had a great impression of me when I arrived.

Interestingly enough, this all became apparent to me several years later when I left the organization. I was about to transition to another new leadership role in a new organization in a new city. At one of the last lunches I enjoyed with my team, they let me know, in a humorous and light-hearted way, that their first impressions of me years ago were not great. Apparently, I seemed overconfident and not super fun to be around. It was a very interesting moment for me, as I know how hard I try to please people all the time. Of course, the words were buffered by the fact that I'd gotten to know these people and knew they all cared about me, but still, that was hard to hear!

The lesson I took from that experience was that you cannot skip those first stages of development from caterpillar to chrysalis when you get to a new place in your leadership journey. Do not be afraid to be vulnerable, ask questions, and learn. You earned your leadership role because you are

BE THE MANATEE

capable and knowledgeable. Give yourself some time to learn about your new place and fill in knowledge gaps. You will exude confidence with your beautiful wings soon enough.

It is important to note that there will be people you meet who do not care for the pattern on your wings no matter what you do. While it is important to develop a working relationship with those you lead and those with whom you collaborate, it is not important that they like you. Your job is to give the best first impression you can, remain teachable, and be your true self, but if that has been done and someone in your organization would rather not chat with you at the water cooler, that does not speak to your competence. So, give them space, move forward with kindness, and confidently flap your wings.

Take Time to Reflect

- What changes in yourself have you noticed as you developed your leadership skills and leadership style? Consider the last time you entered a new role and how you felt when meeting new people or starting a new project.

- Does it seem that those around you are sometimes intimidated by you? What might you be doing that causes this intimidation?

- **Challenge:** Consider one specific instance in which you think you may have flapped your butterfly wings in a way that frightened or annoyed someone. Jot down some ideas about how you can resolve any lingering or future conflicts related to your beautiful, flapping wings.

- **Making Progress:** What do you need? Whose help do you need to get there?

_____

_____

_____

_____

_____

_____

_____

_____

_____

_____

_____

BE THE MANATEE

PART II

Leading
Others

Asking questions and taking note of
reactions by your supervisors or experienced
peers in new situations does not evoke
incompetence but rather conscientiousness.

THE BOWERBIRD

*What if I am a new leader or
new to my organization?*

So, you attained a new leadership position. Likely, you did so, in part, because you know a lot. Perhaps you have a great deal of experience within your field. Perhaps you earned one or more advanced degrees relevant to the position. However you obtained your knowledge, you are here, and you are ready to apply it. It's an exciting moment when you finally get to show what you know and lead those around you to the next phase of growth and greatness.

However, there are scenarios where you may find your knowledge is high, but you are new to an organization. Eager to apply your knowledge, you may make mistakes when you make a shift or change before learning the organizational processes necessary for success. You may find that there is still quite a bit that you did not, or even could not, know when you walked in the door for the first day on the job.

Through these scenarios, you may feel frustrated because you want to exude confidence and competence, and yet there are elements of your job that you simply do not know and must now learn. Experienced leaders in the organization around you may have a deep understanding of the culture in your new place of work and strong relationships with stakeholders–and now, you have to fit in. These situations may result in counterproductive reactions, such as anxiety, frustration, or feeling like a fraud.

Soon after I finished my doctorate, I changed jobs from one leadership role to another but within a new organization. On paper, I had the skills and knowledge to make an impact, and yet I found myself occasionally stuck without an answer when faced with a new, difficult, or new and difficult situation. I remember one day during my first year at my new job, my boss and I were faced with a particularly unhappy client. They were angry about a legal policy reinforced by the board that I was powerless to change even if I wanted to. As a result of this policy, they were also angry at people within my building and were becoming angry with my boss and me as we explained the importance of said policy. I had to both support this immovable policy and move to a solution with an angry person standing in front of me.

As previously mentioned, I am a people pleaser at heart. It is just part of who I am, for better or worse. I am capable of making tough decisions, but my mental default is to make the person in front of me happy when I do not know what to do otherwise. So, I was faced with a new and difficult situation in which my default setting of making the person happy was not going to be helpful, as it would have gone against a policy I was professionally (and, in this case, legally) bound to uphold. My degrees did not matter at this point.

Do we kick this person out of the building for being angry? Do we just show them in the procedure guide where we are obligated to follow this rule? Do we just apologize a lot until they leave? This was a pure moment of needing to apply experience that I did not have. My boss had this experience, however, and I watched as she deftly handled this person's concerns with both compassion and steadfastness. She let them vent their anger, listened to the root of their concerns, and then addressed those roots as opposed to arguing or simply saying, "Too bad."

From that experience, I gained confidence that I would know what to say the next time someone approached me with opinions or concerns on matters outside of my control. I saw my boss face an angry person and saw that she was okay afterward, which made me feel like I would be okay if that happened to me in the future. It was a very valuable moment through which I was reminded of the bowerbird.

The bowerbird is an Australian bird, and the male of the species attracts a mate by adorning their nests with decorative items such as berries and shells.[6] The male bowerbird will sometimes steal items from other nests if they see something they feel would make a nice addition to their own. If a female bowerbird finds a male's nest satisfactory, she will choose him as a mate (see Footnote 6). For the male bowerbird, taking the time to find the best adornments for his nest is rewarded. Taken one step further, this ritual is pivotal for the survival of the species.

I remember being in a meeting, at one point in a previous position, and listening to a very experienced leader give advice to new leaders in the organization. Coincidentally, these new leaders were moving into the exact position I eventually held when I found myself in the predicament described above. The leader's advice resonated with me, and I'll never forget it. He said to watch the experienced leaders around you when they make decisions. He said that new leaders are faced with uncomfortable decisions every day. He said to trust the experienced leaders around you, as they have likely made that same decision many times and have the tools to navigate any variation of the decision point that may come their way.

I did not realize it at the time, but what he was truly saying was to collect every moment of experience dropped by experienced leaders around us and adorn our metaphorical nest with those experiences. Our gathering will not only be rewarded but is critical to future success.

Your nest adornments may come in the form of learning the importance and influence of specific stakeholders in your community, learning procedures and policies, troubleshooting new proprietary technology, or any number of other things. In my case, I was able to gather experiences from a senior leader who directly supervised me. If you are the senior leader and you are new to the role, seek out a mentor. Ask questions, observe their behavior, and watch for their approach and execution of decisions.

Perhaps you are not a new leader but have a great amount of experience. Remember that those around you are watching and "collecting" your experience. Embrace this and develop those around you because leadership development in others can ensure the success of your organization after you retire or leave. Does that mean you have to be perfect? No. But do not be afraid to pull in your rising leaders on the team and discuss the reasons behind certain decisions, or allow them to observe you while making critical decisions or applying your experience. Give your future leaders something shiny to add to their nests!

Asking questions and taking note of the reactions of your supervisors or experienced peers in new situations does not evoke incompetence but rather conscientiousness. Even if you technically have more degrees or specific expertise than your supervisor, that does not directly equate to the capacity to effectively navigate difficult decisions or scenarios. The key is to watch and listen carefully, then hold on to that knowledge. Use it to adorn your nest so that the next time the situation arises, you know what to do. As you perform tasks and learn your role, opportunities to move or improve your organization will likely result in a more successful outcome because your academic knowledge will now be combined with procedural and organizational knowledge. You not only know what to do but how to do it.

Carla's Response

I was so excited to be appointed to my first position as a district leader. My boss and my boss's boss had selected me for the role from a fairly large and diverse pool of applicants. I felt wanted and even loved.

My colleagues were smart and good at their jobs. I was surrounded by people who were willing to guide me, teach me, and help me. My leaders and colleagues had lots of knowledge and experience. They shared it with me freely, and I gathered up their collection of adornments to start building my own leadership nest.

Six months later, my boss retired. I was just crushed. Then a new boss was appointed to lead our team in a completely different style. There was a new opportunity to watch and learn, and I collected more adornments to add to my leadership nest. Eventually, I was ready to take my adornments and make a move. I started watching for other positions to open in other divisions of the organization. I applied and was selected for a new position. I began working hard to learn a completely new job and the new people with whom I now worked. I noted that camaraderie was strong among the team, the work ethic was excellent, and the team's boss was extremely knowledgeable. As Sarah suggested, I quickly realized my boss, and her number two, had a lot to teach me. They were excellent teachers. They were open to the many questions I had and spent the time needed to teach and guide me. I learned many new skills that I have used in each leadership role I have held since that time.

When I first arrived at the new job, I was uncomfortable because it was different from anything I had ever done. I lacked some of the skills I needed for the new job. However, the environment—their nest—was so beautifully adorned with helpmates, technology, tools, and opportunities to learn and grow that I was on the steepest growth curve I had ever experienced. I worked hard and put in long hours and was rewarded in many ways. I valued the many new things I learned, and there were so many benefits, or adornments, if you will, that I stayed for several years. Then, when it was time for my next step in leadership, I was prepared with a beautifully adorned nest of my own.

I agree with Sarah that it is important to learn from your senior leaders when you land a new leadership position. It is critical to watch closely and listen carefully to what the senior leaders do and how they do it. Observe how they prioritize their tasks. It is valuable to listen to how they talk to their employees and their clients. It is helpful to pay attention to their approach to their job. Be aware of their attitude toward the work and the people. Notice what time they arrive at work and what time they leave at the end of the day. Pay attention to when they take a vacation and how they take care of themselves. Use your own critical thinking skills to help you discern what traits of your senior leaders you want to emulate. As you help your senior leaders adorn the nest with the skills and talents you brought with you in the first place and those new skills and talents you are learning from them, they will likely appreciate your contributions to the team and what you have added to the nest. Be the bowerbird and help make the nest attractive. That will likely draw new people to the team who are looking for a beautiful nest, a good place to work and grow, and you will no longer be the new kid on the team but rather a continuously growing leader.

Take Time to Reflect

- Are you new (or newer) to your leadership position? What strengths do you bring to the table? In what areas do you lack experience?

- Write about a moment when you truly did not know how to handle a new situation. Did an experienced leader lend some experience that you could take with you? What did you learn?

- **Challenge:** Keep a running list of the bits of experience and tools that you pick up from those around you as you learn a new role. List them here or keep a notebook. Physically writing these experiences can help you retain them, and you can refer to them later if needed.

- **Making Progress:** What do you need? Whose help do you need to get there?

_____

_____

_____

_____

_____

_____

_____

_____

_____

_____

_____

BE THE MANATEE

To build a diverse, vibrant, and cohesive team, remember the capybara and be willing to spend time with those who feel differently than you.

THE CAPYBARA

What if the people I work with
think differently than me?

Throughout my career as an educator, I've maintained a pretty firm personal philosophy to never let a student or parent leave a conversation frustrated or upset. I have approached situations in which a "customer" was dissatisfied and set my mind with positive intentions throughout these conversations. For example, if a student approached me about an unsatisfactory grade, I not only took the time to answer questions or provide further feedback, but I also made sure the student had a plan of action to improve their grade. An angry parent, furious over a discipline referral, would often end the phone call as a partner with me on the journey to help their student make positive adjustments to their behavior.

As I moved into leadership roles in educational organizations, I maintained this philosophy and extended it to those for whom I served as an administrator. Difficult conversations happened with those on the team, but a plan for change was always the goal. It was challenging, however, when my philosophies did not match those around me in the workplace. Layers of complication are added to difficult conversations when moral, political, ethical, and spiritual beliefs collide. Parents and students have these beliefs as well, but coworkers and colleagues hold a different place in an educational leader's organization. They are not the client; they are the team. And a school or district team must get along despite a lot of differences that may exist beyond the commonality of educating children.

I experienced such a collision of beliefs early in my career as a leader. A faculty member disagreed with a district policy and struggled to implement it, resulting in an email from me with a friendly reminder to hop back on the right track. The morning after the aforementioned email was sent, she entered my office. Quiet at first, she was appreciative of the reminder and agreeable to making a change but made a quick pivot to express how frustrated she was that the policy did not mesh with some of her personal beliefs. It is likely not an uncommon situation for an employee to disagree with a rule and for the leader of the organization to enforce the rule under the pretense of their position. The tough part in my scenario was navigating the fact that I did not share the personal beliefs that contributed to her objection.

My job at that moment was not to change her heart or mind. Her beliefs were her own as mine were my own. Rather, as is the case for many organizational leaders, the policy was mandatory from a high level within the organization, and nothing I said or did could change that. So, I remained transparent and open about the reasoning behind the policy and asked how I could support her. As a result, she felt heard, as she was able to express her opinion, and from that day on, she did not struggle with implementing the policy.

You will notice that I did not share my opposing personal beliefs with her, and I can assure you that it was not for lack of passion about the issue. I did not talk about my beliefs in an effort to play devil's advocate or encourage her to explore another perspective. That was not required here and would likely have brought further frustration. She left my office knowing nothing of my inner thoughts and everything about the support I could offer.

I am not suggesting losing your sense of self when you become a leader or disregarding the beliefs of others. Instead, think of yourself as a sounding board, a place to be a listener. It does not mean you will agree with every person you work with or for, but it will mean that those around you may find that you provide a safe space. This safe space is invaluable because, in order to move an organization forward, cohesive teams must exist despite differing, or even conflicting, belief systems.

While researching for this book, I happened upon many delightful images of the capybara, a large rodent native to Central and South America. A capybara looks like an overgrown beaver, sans paddle tail, and is about the size of a Labrador Retriever. What made these images particularly delightful is the tendency for other animals, such as birds and monkeys, to take a seat on the capybara's back while it crosses a river or takes a nap on the shore. Calm and unbothered, the capybara continues on its way while supporting others for a rest or movement forward.[7]

The capybara offers an excellent example of the mentality to take when working with someone who carries different moral, political, religious, educational, or leadership philosophies than you. The capybara does not attempt to dissuade the bird from taking a rest on its back. It simply carries the bird across the river to the other side. Think of your next initiative within your organization or the next policy with which you are charged with implementing. People on your team may not agree on how to move forward. People on your team may have philosophical differences with the policy.

I find the lesson of the capybara can be helpful even in situations where the stakes are much lower than who you vote for, where you worship, or where you stand on the scope and sequence of teaching reading fundamentals. For example, I have found myself in several leadership situations where the team members I serve have vastly different tastes than my own in music, movies, and ideas in regard to what constitutes a good time on the weekend.

However, by embracing the mindset of the capybara and finding serenity in the company of different individuals, I found that conversations led to quality friendships among my teammates. We could not rely on surface-level topics for conversation but rather looked deeper for common ground and developed a mutual respect for our varying tastes and ideas. One friend in particular comes to mind, as we truly found ourselves to be opposites in most facets of our lives. It became a running joke because one of us liking something almost guaranteed that the other would not. Yet, we cared about each other, we supported each other's work, and our differences were a joy, even if we felt strongly about them, because we cared more for each other than those things. We loved working together, even if we would never have the same pick for a Friday night movie.

I would be remiss to close this chapter without reminding you to be proud of who you are. Have friends outside of work who see you and love you. Vote in every election as you feel convicted to vote. Go to the music concerts that bring your soul to life. You don't have to worry about liking the same stuff as those around you or holding the same personal beliefs and values. You do not have to fit a certain mold. But to build a diverse, vibrant, and cohesive team, remember the capybara and be willing to spend time with those who feel differently than you. This may help drive your vision and mission forward.

Carla's Response

As Sarah mentioned, the capybara serves other animals by allowing them to perch on its back while it transports them where they want to go. Consequently, the capybara has no problem making friends with animals of other species. It is also willing to share its habitat with other animals. While the capybara is the largest rodent in the world, it is peaceful, relaxed in their manner, and sociable. It spends time playing with other animals and even cuddling with various species.

I do not consider myself to be relaxed but rather intense at times about work. However, I do seem to attract people, similar to the way the capybara attracts other animals. This trait has served me well in my career of serving and leading people. I am willing to help people with their work, help them understand new ideas, and even carry them along like the capybara carries animals across the water. People respond well to genuine kindness in the form of help and support.

After I retired from my leadership role in a very large public school district, I took on a leadership role at a university renowned for its Educational Leadership program. In this role, I worked with graduate and post-graduate students who were seeking formal leadership roles in various organizations and some who were already serving in leadership roles. As the leader of the faculty, I also worked closely with about thirty instructors. Faculty members and I engaged our students in an annual doctoral research symposium, an event that enriched their journey while they were studying with us. University leaders decided to pilot an award program for outstanding doctoral dissertations, and they decided students could nominate themselves for these awards. The director of the award program was overwhelmed with a surprisingly large number of applications for outstanding dissertation awards. During a planning meeting, the director said to me, "Carla, I now realize that your students do whatever you tell them to do." She was referencing the disproportionately high number of students from the program I was leading who had both submitted proposals to be presenters at the symposium and applied for awards. I reflected on why that was the case. I determined a few things were at play that resulted in such a high level of engagement among my students. One important factor was that I communicated often and clearly the expectation to participate in the symposium and the benefits of doing so. That was not the only factor, though. I also determined it was because I had created relationships with the students across the program. When I taught them, I started each class with upbeat music to raise the energy level among the students. I also demonstrated a sense of humor in the class polls I presented at the beginning of each class to help set a frame of mind for the time we would spend together doing rigorous work. I sent regular emails and text messages to students, offering encouragement and celebratory comments for small successes throughout their graduate student journey. I even developed little running jokes with some students to keep their spirits high while studying complex matters. Like the capybara, I displayed a relaxed manner despite the intensity of the work we were doing, and I was sociable in a way that was personable and respectful. It helped the students want to do what I was guiding them through, so they could reach their own goals of attaining higher education degrees and leadership roles in their careers.

My leadership takeaways from this experience were fourfold. First, the well-known fact that the teacher–student relationship is the most influential factor in student success applies not only to children but also to adult students and their teacher, me. Second, clear communication of expectations leads to high levels of engagement. Third, the use of humor goes a long way toward helping people to want to do what you are saying and doing. And finally, establishing an environment that is welcoming and positive supports engagement and success.

Take Time to Reflect

- Have you ever been the one in the room that felt the opposite of everyone else? How did that feel?

- How have you, or perhaps a leader you have worked for, worked to build a cohesive team?

- **Challenge:** Think of the person on your team with whom you share the least in common. Do you have a good working relationship with this person? How can you work together to find some common ground to move the team's work forward?

- **Making Progress:** What do you need? Whose help do you need to get there?

_____

_____

_____

_____

_____

_____

_____

_____

_____

_____

_____

_____

BE THE MANATEE

Make sure your own emotions are in check so you can help others manage their emotions.

THE ELEPHANT

How can I ensure harmony at work?

I have worked under the leadership of many exemplary educators. Some of them demonstrated the qualities of the elephant. An elephant herd is typically made up of six to twelve elephants, and the leader of the herd is the oldest and wisest female. The lead elephant does not dominate but, instead, leads. She does so with wisdom, strength, and skills such as problem-solving, openness, patience, confidence, and compassion.[8] The other elephants depend on her to make decisions, and they follow her by literally walking in a line behind her, single file. Elephants are very intelligent and carry crucial information for survival, using their long-term memory, such as where they previously saw food and water resources. When comparing the elephant leader to a human leader, the trait of openness can improve the lives of a herd of elephants or a group of team members. Elephant leaders use the attribute of patience to think things over and respond to circumstances with calmness. They tend to demonstrate confidence and remain steadfast with their decisions.

Elephants are particularly attentive to the needs of their young. Like human babies, elephant babies are born with little or no survival instincts and rely on their mothers and relatives to teach them how to survive (see Footnote 8). Additionally, elephants demonstrate care for all members of the herd, showing that each member is valued.[9] According to Sommer,[10] elephants form strong bonds with others, mourn and grieve, and the lead elephant focuses on balancing the needs of all the members in their herd, including details, such as food, safety, and caring for the young.

It seems that humans and some wild animals have the same expectations of their leaders—someone they can trust to keep them safe, who has their back, and who has the best interest of the group at heart.[11] I have worked with several educational leaders who exhibited these traits, building trust with me and others.

One of My Favorite Leaders

I was teaching high school. The principal of the school was beloved by all. During our first faculty meeting of the year on a day of pre-planning, he announced that he had been offered and accepted a promotion in the school district and would be leaving our high school to serve as an area director. The faculty members were devastated, and we began the students' first day of school without a principal. It took weeks, even months, for district leaders to determine a suitable replacement principal. She finally arrived late in the fall.

The new principal, whom I will call Dr. Z, had a hard act to follow, so the chances of successful leadership were not in her favor. During her first day at a school I truly enjoyed, a campus inspector arrived before lunch and noticed there were soda machines and snack machines scattered about the campus for student use, a feature of the school I thought helped make each day go more smoothly. The inspector arrived before lunch and declared a policy violation because vending machines cannot be available to students prior to the lunch serving times in the cafeteria. Apparently, there was a little-known policy prohibiting any competition with the federally-funded school breakfast and lunch program. Dr. Z knew about this policy, but since it was her first day on campus, she did not realize the vending machines were all over the school and open for students to use throughout the day. She immediately had all the vending machines locked until all lunch sessions were over every day for the rest of her tenure at the school. What a meanie she seemed to be!

Creating Harmony

Little did the faculty know that she had the leadership skills of the elephant. One of the first things she did after that first day of acclimation and seeming crisis was to visit teachers in their classrooms during their planning time to get to know each one of us. She visited when classes were full of students as well. I was teaching journalism at the time. My class of students, who were responsible for researching, writing, and publishing the school newspaper, were curious about the new principal who had taken away their access to food goodies. The students wanted to write a feature story about Dr. Z. I shared that idea with her, and she came to meet my journalism students and offered herself up to the students for them to ask her questions with no restrictions. As a former journalism teacher herself, Dr. Z seemed excited and happy to be in my journalism classroom. I will never forget the moment when *Bobby* asked her, "Since nobody likes you, what are you going to do about that?" Dr. Z glanced my way–I wanted to crawl under my desk. But she chuckled and began her response. She shared with the students that she did not realize nobody liked her, and now that she knew this fact, she was going to work to gain their trust. She explained the details behind the reason for locking the vending machines. She took the time to listen to the students and answered all their questions in detail.

Later, she confided in me that Bobby's question was a bit painful, but she understood why students would feel antagonistic toward her. After all, she had replaced a principal everyone loved and limited their access to snacks! Not a great start. Nevertheless, Dr. Z gained the trust of faculty and students by being honest and transparent, promoting peace and harmony, and genuinely caring for others.

During Dr. Z's seven-year tenure at the school, I had what felt like a crisis. My students had begun to win local, state, and national awards for their journalistic endeavors, and our school newspaper was ranked among the best in the state. The students and I were gaining confidence and pride in our work. They were writing about more complex and meaningful topics than they had previously. Whenever teenagers decide to write about important issues, journalism teachers must brace themselves for the reader reactions that inevitably follow. The editor of the school newspaper, my student, wrote a story on an important topic, and we published it. One of the faculty members was offended by the editor's article and attacked me in writing. He accused me of prejudice as well as poor teaching practices. Prior to that, a different teacher made similarly negative comments about the student publication and blamed me. I learned about his accusations when another teacher found his written letter about me in the faculty copy machine. In fact, he had left it there while the school was being used as a hurricane shelter for community members! I had no way of knowing who or how many people had read these accusations against me.

I was absolutely crushed. I went to Dr. Z to let her know I had been wrongly accused and in a potentially public way because of the multiple copies of the written letter being left around during a time when community members were on campus. She called a meeting with the teacher, who had accused me, one of the assistant principals, and me. She restored harmony. I was amazed at how she handled my emotions, how she managed the meeting, and the outcome. It turned out that Dr. Z was a resonant leader: "Resonant leaders are in tune with those around them. This results in people working in sync with each other...In addition to knowing and managing themselves well, emotionally intelligent leaders manage others' emotions and build strong, trusting relationships."[12]

Eventually, Dr. Z solidified her relationship with me further. Not only did Dr. Z support the publication and the editor's article, but she developed a little inside joke with me that went something like this: "Carla, if only you knew what you were doing…" She knew that I had been hurt and discouraged when my colleagues criticized my ability to teach well. Dr. Z meant her statement to encourage me to march forward and keep on making good things happen for and with my students. She continued to make that same statement to me every time my students or I accomplished something meaningful. She consistently employed the practices of a resonant leader: "Resonant leaders manage their emotions well and read individuals and groups accurately. They consciously attune to people, focus them on a common cause, build a sense of community, and create a climate that enables people to tap into passion, energy, and a desire to move together in a positive direction," (see Footnote 12). Not only did my principal encourage me, but she connected to my feelings, helped me handle them, encouraged me to work creatively and passionately with my students, and restored a sense of community among the faculty.

Over time, I observed Dr. Z demonstrate her commitment to protecting the students and preserving a harmonious school climate. One day, there was a crisis in the kitchen of the school cafeteria. One of my students came running into my journalism classroom, proclaiming I needed to see what the principal was doing, and a camera was needed to photograph her. It turned out that the principal was standing in the food serving area of the cafeteria, donning a hair net and plastic gloves as she served up plate after plate of food for the students. There was a problem in the kitchen, but she made sure the children were fed. I often saw her after school with a pressure washer assisting the custodial staff in cleaning the sidewalk and patio. I saw her water plants growing around campus. I walked into a meeting after school one day and found Dr. Z rolling a pile of quarters. I looked at her inquisitively, and she simply said, "Don't even ask." She was clearly filling in the gap for a club on campus that was engaged in a fundraiser, and the club sponsor was unable to secure the money collected that day. Again, she made sure the children were cared for and the teachers were supported, even if that meant rolling coins.

Eventually, Dr. Z moved on to a district leadership position, retired, then returned to teach students who were incarcerated. She is one of the finest leaders I have ever known and a truly good person. My leadership takeaways from my time spent with Dr. Z were simple and powerful–take time to listen to the people you lead, make sure your own emotions are in check so you can help others manage their emotions, make sure the children are safe and fed, and create harmony among your team.

Sarah's Response

As I read about Carla's description of a resonant and servant leader, I am reminded of a time when I was led by those who provided excellent examples of what not to do. I remember what it felt like to follow those leaders as part of the herd but being unsure of the final destination and not feeling secure on the journey to get there.

While there is no need to go into great detail for the sake of anonymity, the leaders under whom I've served, who did not exemplify the characteristics of a matriarchal elephant, had some qualities in common. First, there was an unwillingness to serve. I've been through many leadership seminars, meetings, conferences, and graduate programs, and the message of servant leadership rings throughout each one. If you are not willing to roll up your sleeves and get your hands dirty in the work, why would people do it for you? I'm not saying to avoid delegating tasks, empowering future leaders, or distributing your leadership among a team. I'm simply saying that when your organization needs all-hands-on-deck, I found, in my professional experience, it did not sit well for the leader to avoid the mess.

Second, these leaders showed a lack of courage. Leadership is not for the faint of heart, and facing serious issues takes guts to resolve. It's uncomfortable when staff are divided over significant professional issues, but the leader must guide them through it. It can be painful and frustrating when results do not line up with the desired expectations, but the leader must stay positive, have some grace, and start building competency and confidence. I've seen a range of responses from inactivity to questionable ethics in response to a crisis. A lack of elephant-like characteristics, indeed.

If you find yourself in a situation with a decidedly un-elephant-like leader, remember to stay true to your values and committed to your profession, as I can tell you that you will likely not remain under that leadership forever. Take the lessons on what not to do and remember them if faced with difficulty on your leadership path. When in doubt, think of the elephant and take care of your herd.

Take Time to Reflect

- Do you know anyone like Dr. Z? Think about the best leader you know. What character traits do they have that you wish to emulate and develop in your character?

- Think about a time you have seen a leader respond to a crisis effectively. How did they harmoniously move the team through the crisis?

- **Challenge:** Consider some of the most rewarding professional relationships you have had. What about those relationships made them so satisfying? How can you implement those components into your own leadership style? Write them down.

- **Making Progress:** What do you need? Whose help do you need to get there?

_____

_____

_____

_____

_____

_____

_____

_____

_____

_____

BE THE MANATEE

*Being flexible does not mean making a
sacrifice to your core leadership values.*

From Sarah's Experience

THE OCTOPUS

*What if the people I serve respond
to different leadership styles?*

I remember the first day of my first year as a teacher. I taught eighth-grade American History and seventh-grade geography. My degree, the diploma that had barely lived in its frame for a summer, was in teaching the social sciences to secondary-level students with a focus on American History. I interned for an entire semester and had hours of observation in previous terms. If ever a degree prepared an individual for the workplace, this was it.

The first day came and went. I introduced myself to my students, let them know what the class would be about this year, talked them through my expectations, and reviewed the sundry forms and pamphlets required by my administrators. We worked through presentations and assignments, I gave homework, and some of them returned it. I quickly realized that once the honeymoon phase of the new year ended, the students' personalities began to shine, and nothing in my training prepared me for working with students wired so differently than me. *What do you mean you simply refuse to do your homework?*

Sure, my education provided knowledge of the social sciences, which came in handy while discussing content, and I had a general understanding of child psychology to handle a teenager's mood swing, but in the moment of a student's meltdown, refusal, or looking at a sea of bored faces, I felt like I knew absolutely nothing. I had to learn to think on my feet and accept these wonderfully and wildly different teenagers for who they were and teach the way they needed me to teach, not the way I read about or the way that I needed when I was a student. At first, I felt like I was sacrificing something, like I was giving up what I knew good teaching to be. But the truth is, good teaching is the kind of teaching that gets kids learning and gets kids engaged, so they remember the learning. I found that my core value as a teacher did not actually change, just my approach. Customization and differentiation were the keys.

In the years since, as I've moved along in my career and my own education, I've sat in a lot of training for people in leadership roles. I have read books, written papers, and participated in classes centered solely on leadership skills and navigating challenges. I learned about delegating and distributive leadership. I learned about being compassionate and yet holding expectations. Once again, I had lots of training for my new job roles. Yet, I found that my new supervisory roles often left me feeling like I did as a first-year teacher, realizing that not every student will tackle school like I did, because the truth is the adults I lead won't necessarily respond to leadership the same way I do either. I also believe this is true for leadership positions in any field or organization, not just education.

There are animals in the wild well adapted to change based on their environment. One such animal, and one of the most fascinating creatures in the ocean, in my opinion, is the octopus. These cephalopods are masters of camouflage. Like a chameleon, an octopus can change colors to blend in with its surroundings, but the octopus takes this ability one step further, as some species can change their skin texture to look like coral or rock in order to hide from predators or stalk prey.[13] The Mimic Octopus can even adjust its colors, shape, and movements to look like other sea creatures (see Footnote 13)!

The octopus offers an important piece of advice for an inexperienced leader or leader in a new position or organization—even if you never change internally, sometimes you have to change your approach in order to achieve the best result. In one situation, an octopus may need to shape its body like coral and take on the color to match; while on other days, the need may arise to be as smooth and gray as a rock on the seafloor. The point is, the octopus is flexible but at the end of the day, it is still an octopus. Just because you delegate one task but collaborate on another does not mean you are sacrificing your core values as a leader.

As a leader in my field, I have had the privilege of working with smart, capable teams. Up until a couple of years ago, I found that it was adequate to delegate a task to a team member, give some time, and then check in on their progress and see if any assistance was needed–typical stuff, no need to change the formula. However, on one occasion, a particular project came along where I found my usual approach to delegation rebuffed. A check-in felt cursory at best and sometimes just uncomfortable as it was clear that, frankly, the team did not need me in order to complete the project. Like, at all.

Was I losing my touch? Was I unhelpful? Was I sacrificing a core value of leadership in which I offered assistance as much as possible?

No. No to all of those things. Just because my team did not need me to complete a project did not mean I was ineffective in my position or not needed in other aspects of our work together. They just didn't need me for that project because they were more than capable of handling it and did an outstanding job. And I mean, as leaders, is that not what we want? I was left grappling with feeling unneeded but realized I was still an octopus–I just had to change my approach to the necessary camouflage.

Some time went by, and opportunities brought me to a new team with whom I greatly enjoyed my time. A project came along, a team member took the lead on it, and I was asked to supervise the effort. Having experienced the aforementioned situation in which independence was valued over assistance, I let this person go about making the project happen. I knew the perfect camouflage for this particular area of the seafloor. This team member was (and is) a very talented person who successfully handled their job on a daily basis, much like the people on my former team. However, this particular project, while successful in some ways, missed the mark in others once it was finished.

But how? It turned out that I fell into the trap again of applying the same approach to different people. I chose the wrong camouflage and was left looking like a big lump of pink coral when other textures and colors were called for. When debriefing the project, this person and I realized that they had wanted more check-ins throughout the entire process. They felt like they needed more help.

An important lesson smacked me right in the face during that meeting. I could have saved myself a lot of trouble in both scenarios, with my independent team and my more collaborative team member, by simply asking what kind of leadership they needed from me throughout the duration of the project. By asking that question on day one of the project, as opposed to realizing what was needed after the fact, I could have taken the guesswork out of my leadership approach.

As an important note for someone whose brain works like mine, with situations involving very independent teams, it became essential for me to distinguish between feelings of effectiveness and feelings of acceptance. If I am tasked with supervising a team, and they only need me occasionally to be successful, as long as I do my part to assist when they need me, I am still effective even if I am not present during late-night planning sessions. And if I am left out of the actual creation of a project, it does not mean my team doesn't like me.

On the flip side, if feelings of acceptance are not a factor for you within your work, it may become necessary for you to be willing to jump in and

BE THE MANATEE

help if you find yourself working with someone who needs more hands-on collaboration from their leader. Just because they need you more than others does not make them less capable than someone who can go off on their own. It is not a personality flaw or being needy if your team member requires more of your time to get something done.

I vowed to ask my teams what kind of leadership they needed on projects from then on because I knew that I had the tools to differentiate. However, predicting the correct tool to use can be difficult in a particular situation because every person, much like my students, may need something different to get the job done. If the person or team is unsure of the leadership style they need, you can agree to remain flexible. Being flexible does not mean making a sacrifice to your core leadership values. You're still you, as the octopus is still an octopus. You're just making sure you are taking on the right camouflage to be successful.

Carla's Response

Sarah's important point about customizing your leadership strategies to best serve your team really struck a chord with me. I am thinking about a time when I did customize my approach and another time when I should have done that.

I had just been appointed to oversee a new initiative that was important to many stakeholders. The initiative was very high-profile, and I provided support, training, oversight, and legal compliance with leaders at more than ten schools. I worked intensively with principals at two of those schools, and the personalities of those leaders were polar opposites. One principal was jovial, friendly, and outgoing. The other was introverted, quiet, and laser-focused. Both principals were veterans in their role as a principal with a loyal following of teachers who wanted to work with them no matter what school they were leading. I had great respect for them, and I had a lot of work to do at both of their schools with the faculties and the other leaders on the campuses.

The friendly principal typically greeted me with a big smile and said something like, "Where have you been? We have missed you!" Well, I had been there just the day before, as I was on campus almost daily. I learned quickly to stop by the main office and greet everyone there upon each visit. When I left campus, I always poked my head in the office and declared, "Sparks out!"

When I visited the school with the laser-focused principal, I knew this principal was entirely consumed by the safety of the students and the learning that was taking place. The greeting I typically received upon arrival at the campus was a head nod welcoming me to the campus while not breaking stride with the work going on. My customized approach at this school was to check in with the front office secretary, who monitored the coming and going of all visitors. Then, I went about my business of visiting classrooms and meeting with other campus leaders. When my work for the day at that school was done, I quietly slipped out the back gate and went about my other responsibilities. I knew this principal would call me when a discussion or help was needed. I also learned that if I needed her focused attention, I would arrive on campus on Friday afternoon at dismissal time because after the last bus of students and the last car rider left the campus, the principal was all ears and even sociable and personable.

Both these principals needed my support. Their faculties needed my professional development, and they were both entirely capable of running their schools. I often said, "This is your school, and you do not need me to tell you how to run it. However, my program is in your school, and I need to make sure it is successful." Both personality types agreed with me, and this internal drive of mine never changed over the seven years I worked with those principals in my leadership role. However, externally, I made sure I was the colorful, coral-type octopus at one school while I was the sleek, camouflaged octopus at the other school. I was still an octopus at both schools, and I was good at customizing and differentiating my approach to meet the needs of each principal.

There was another time when I failed to recognize the talent and skill of a teacher leader and did not customize my approach. A small group of teacher leaders had approached me with a grand idea to initiate a huge but short-term initiative. They convinced me to take the lead and became my go-to people, my guiding team.

One of these teacher leaders has the greatest strength I have ever seen in the ability to work smarter, not harder. I have seen her time and time again accomplish a task in just a short half hour or so that would take me hours or even days to finish because she knows how to find help, delegate, oversee, and move on to the next thing. I, on the other hand, typically take the approach of the bigger the job, the harder I work. Hmmm...

While working on the intense short-term initiative, I held regular weekly check-ins with my guiding team. During one of those weeks, our task was to prepare beautiful portfolios with logos on the front by filling them with important materials in a specific order to be distributed at the opening event of the big initiative. I had left all the portfolios and other materials with the skillful teacher leader because we were going to meet at her school that afternoon to complete the task. When I arrived, all the portfolios were stuffed with materials and stacked neatly, ready to use. I should have been excited, but I was quite dismayed. Well, that seems to be a ridiculous reaction, but the truth was she had altered my plan for the meeting by being so efficient, and she had ordered the materials differently than what I had in mind. It really bugged me at first. Looking back, I should have given her high praise and learned from her skill. To my credit, I eventually recognized her level of efficiency and gave her the space she needed to independently accomplish important and *time-consuming tasks without my interference. Where I had initially been stubborn and hindered by the negative side of perfectionism, I became willing to change my approach without changing my core leadership values.*

Take Time to Reflect

- Think about a time when your help was exactly what someone needed to succeed. How did you feel?

- Think about a time when you were completely unhelpful or unnecessary to your team in order to complete a project—perhaps you were in a leadership position or not. What was that experience like for you? How do you feel about taking a step back as your team works?

- **Challenge:** The next time you lead a team, ask them up-front how they would like to be led. A fifteen-minute standing meeting once a week? Hour-long collaboration sessions? Channel the octopus and adjust your leadership for the needs of your team.

- **Making Progress:** What do you need? Whose help do you need to get there?

_____

_____

_____

_____

_____

_____

_____

_____

_____

_____

BE THE MANATEE

BE THE MANATEE

PART III

Avoiding
Toxic
Behavior

*Leaders must understand what they can
do and cannot do to change a situation.*

THE WOLF

How do I avoid fostering distrust in my organization?

During the breeding season, gray wolves are not exactly what we call faithful in their relationships.[14] Gray wolves will find a mate but continue to reproduce with other wolves without regard for loyalty. While gray wolves are social animals that live and hunt in packs, they are predators.[15] In the case of human leadership, the traits of the gray wolf are divisive and harmful, in my experience.

I would compare the gray wolf to colleagues and leaders who are intimidating but know how to create friendships at work. They are relational and predatory all at once. That can be a dangerous combination of character traits to navigate for novice administrators who are assigned to work with people who are like the gray wolf. Imagine a leader, perhaps your colleague or even your boss, who seems friendly and makes overtures to develop a friendship with you. Then as you, the novice leader, begin to trust your colleague or boss, he preys on you. At first, he gives you his work to do on top of your own work. You know he likes you, so you accept the additional workload despite realizing the tasks involved are not part of your job. Then eventually, your boss lets out a big wolf howl, which is a method of communication, and calls for another colleague to enter the scene. You are now cast aside until your skills are needed again.

Facing the Gray Wolf

In my first role as a formal leader, I had a wonderful boss, and then he suddenly retired six months after he hired me. One of my colleagues was promoted to the boss position. I was happy for my colleague. Soon, this person began building upon the friendship we had begun to establish as members of the same team. The new boss made me feel needed and valued. Yet, there were intense moments when I felt overwhelmed by the work the new boss gave me to do. Unbeknownst to me, the boss was doing the same thing with the other team members. The boss began confiding in me about things he did not like or appreciate about my colleagues. While that bothered me, I figured he needed a confidant, and I was the person in whom he chose to confide because I am a good listener. Eventually, he began telling me things I should not have known, such as how he intentionally made a colleague feel bad to teach them a lesson. He even went so far as to tell me he was going to remove a colleague from the team so he could make an example of that person to get everyone else in line. I was shocked and even frightened to hear these things.

I agonized over the secret knowledge I carried and did not know what to do with it since my boss counted on me to help him. I did not realize that the boss was talking similarly to my colleagues about me. Oh, if I had only understood that some people lead work teams like gray wolves. They befriend their colleagues and subordinates to exert power over those people. I became wary and watched with unveiled eyes as my boss mistreated each member of our team, including me. I watched him berate individuals during team meetings. I watched him usurp team members' skills. I watched him behave in ways that did not seem professional. I saw all these things happen, but I certainly did not understand what motivated the boss to act this way. Had someone told me there were people in leadership roles with traits similar to gray wolves, I would have at least understood what was happening. Unfortunately, that was not the case, and I was confused. Then I became distraught. I simply did not know what to think, and I certainly did not know what to do about this impossible situation.

Understanding What I Could and Could Not Fix

I traveled with a colleague on the same work team to a national conference in another state. We made a formal presentation. We had known each other for several years and had become friends. She was a wonderful presentation partner whose skill set complemented mine. We enjoyed working together; however, under the leadership of our boss, the same one I described above, my friendship with my teammate had waned. There had never been a confrontation, yet we seemed to be growing apart. I knew she was also being mistreated by our boss, but we had never discussed it. We did not discuss it on that business trip either. However, there was an incredible moment during the evening after our national presentation when we were relaxing and debriefing how the day had gone. At that moment, we caught each other's eye, and without saying anything at all about our boss, we both realized the boss had been talking negatively to each of us about the other. It was a ploy to tear down our work friendship. Why? Who really knows? Perhaps it was a divide-and-conquer approach. If we consider the gray wolf, we know that he is simultaneously a friend and predator and he is not faithful. Those gray wolf traits pretty accurately describe what we were enduring with our boss.

After that business trip, I realized that I would not be able to trust or change my boss's behavior. I tried various approaches to improve the situation and at least learn to cope with it. However, I found myself becoming distressed and even depressed. I finally decided to approach my boss's supervisor. The supervisor was a respected and seasoned leader I had known for a long time, and she had previously invited me to share with her any concerns I had at work. I was not very comfortable approaching her to discuss how my boss was conducting business, but I saw no other option. The supervisor assured me she would address the problem; however, things did not improve at all. Ultimately, I made the agonizing decision to seek a different position and move to a new environment. It took about five months to decide to apply for open positions in other parts of the organization. I absolutely loved the work I was doing, but the environment was toxic and untenable. I was offered the second position for which I applied, and I ran across town to accept it. I no longer had to endure the gray wolf.

While I do not recommend running away from problems as the best approach to solving them, I will admit that, occasionally, the only real solution is to move along to a better situation. The real point I am sharing here is not that you should consider moving to a different position, department, school, or organization. My point is that it is helpful to understand the leadership style and the personality of those who lead you and of yourself. If I had understood my boss better, I might have found another solution to the distress I was feeling and stayed in a position I really liked. My leadership takeaways from this experience were not what my boss taught me but rather that I learned what I could and could not do to change the situation. I could not change my boss's behavior; I tried and failed. I could not control the situation. However, I could manage my emotional reactions to an extent. I could make important decisions about my emotional health and my work environment. I could find a better place to work.

Sarah's Response

At one point in my leadership journey, I worked under a supervisor who managed dozens of individuals. That is a lot of relationship building and a lot of time investing in people. However, as time went by, I began to notice certain behaviors.

This person took more time with some people than others. Their time spent during the workday tended to be around the people who worked on projects where they held more knowledge of the work or with individuals they socialized with outside of the office. I do not initially fault this person for this behavior, especially in the early stages of an organization's development. I tend to stick with who and what I know when I enter a new situation myself. Time moved on, however, and the behavior of this supervisor did not change. For example, if a multi-departmental meeting took place, it was clear which individuals and departments they valued, as they would leave once those departments' portions of the meeting had concluded.

When a project arose in which I was an important part, attention occasionally shifted towards my team and me. I would receive advice, praise, and criticism, all while never hearing a word any other time. I am aware that it may seem obvious in a situation where supervision must be stretched thin that the supervisor has limited ability to spend time with people. A fair thought, but it was still their job to support everyone, and the preference was just so transparent. I was under their supervision for a long time. Their absence was noticed, advice that was received felt hollow, and criticism was not well received because it did not come from a genuine place. How could it? I never saw them outside of the occasional spotlighted project.

I am reminded of the gray wolf because of the shifting loyalty, and I relate to Carla's situation because as time went by, like Carla and her friend at the conference, people started to figure it out. This leader's behavior was observable and negatively affected morale. It is important for leaders to be genuine. It is important for leaders to overcome personal preferences and biases to build a team that feels secure and can thrive, knowing all members have the full support of those who supervise the work. When that support is not felt, a leader may find that people do exactly as Carla felt she had to do–leave.

Take Time to Reflect

- Reflect for a moment on the various leaders with whom you have worked. Consider how their leadership style and personality impacted the people on their team. Consider how they impacted you.

- How would you or did you handle having a friend with traits like the gray wolf? How would you or did you handle having a boss with traits like the gray wolf?

- **Challenge:** Think about your own leadership style. Do you befriend those who look up to you or report to you? How do you treat subordinates–people you lead–whether that be in a formal leadership role or an informal leadership role? How do you want to treat those whom you lead?

- **Making Progress:** What do you need? Whose help do you need to get there?

_____

_____

_____

_____

_____

_____

_____

_____

_____

_____

BE THE MANATEE

BE THE MANATEE

Mosquito bites hurt and itch, and it's hard to forget about them once they are irritated. But they also heal in time.

THE MOSQUITO

*How do I avoid suffering from
negative words and thoughts?*

While the manatee, capybara, and bowerbird all offer model leadership characteristics, another creature provides behavioral examples to be avoided– the mosquito. Mosquitos can be inside a person's mind or within professional relationships. Within your organization, mosquitos are individuals who make a lot of ill-willed buzz in a place of work and have a propensity to metaphorically bite those around them, causing pain and irritation. Therefore, it is critical to identify and learn how to communicate with a mosquito while maintaining distance from the behavior of a mosquito. For mosquitos found in the mind, the ones that cause a loud, annoying buzz in our brains, there is internal work to do.

I've lived in the southeastern United States my entire life, so I can tell you the impact a mosquito has on the well-being of a person ranges from irritating discomfort to intolerable nuisance, depending on the severity of the mosquito attack. According to the Center for Disease Control, a mosquito will bite its prey to consume blood and then inject saliva into the bite. The saliva causes a very itchy reaction that is tough to ignore. To relieve the itch from a mosquito bite, it is important to keep it clean, avoid scratching the bite, and apply treatment if needed. A similar treatment plan can help a leader treat the toxins of a workplace or a mental mosquito.[16]

A colleague of mine worked closely with people who took great pleasure in talking about other people at their place of work–characteristic of a mosquito's buzz. This talk could include insulting things that rarely had roots in a person's professional performance. The desires to fit in and join the gossip were strong. Adding to the gossip got a laugh and a feeling of acceptance, while non-participation was met with feeling left out of the inner circle. My colleague knew the mosquito had bitten her, and the itch, or need to gossip, was tough to ignore.

The problem with this behavior was quickly apparent. Talk can always be overheard. Ears are everywhere, and you never know when someone you believe to be a willing participant in a mosquito's mean-spirited banter is connected to one of the people on the receiving end of the gossip. People were burned by this behavior. Over time, my colleague told me she realized the risk of being left out was also met with a quiet peace in the background of her mind.

After making a conscious decision that she would not participate in the buzz even if it were happening around her, the peace in my colleague's mind grew, and she said it was worth being overlooked for a lunch outing to maintain the knowledge that she was not hurting anyone. People took notice. Her reputation became one of kindness and collaboration. She also told me she began to sleep a lot better.

That's the thing about mosquito bites. They hurt, they itch, and it's hard to forget about them once they are irritated. But they also heal in time. If you find yourself in the presence of a mosquito, someone who is careless with words and buzzing noisily around the workplace, you are always at risk of a bite. But a little prevention in the form of steadfast kindness can help keep lines of communication open while staying out of toxic gossip. Another important note is that you do not need to cut this person(s) out of your life. When you have a conversation, stick to productive talk about work, or simply talk about something else you may have in common—shows you watch, books you read, food, movies, music, etc.

The Buzz From Within

An internal mosquito can be more difficult to eradicate. Despite degrees earned, training experienced, or expertise gained, leaders may face anxiety and imposter syndrome and question their ability to guide and drive their organization. According to the American Psychological Association (APA), imposter syndrome is an inability to accept personal success and a tendency to experience worry over being discovered as some sort of fraud who does not deserve their position.[17] That thought pattern is the buzz of an internal mosquito.

The APA denotes several reasons why an individual might experience imposter syndrome. The accompanying anxiety may result in procrastination, perfectionism, or in my experience, an odd mix of both (see Footnote 17). For example, the buzz of the internal mosquitos I heard, as a new leader in my organization, included an acute awareness of being younger than most of my colleagues, their reactions when I talked about what I knew, as well as a desire to not say anything at all. The frustrations from these thought-based conundrums made me want to hide, show off, quit, cry, and experience lots of complex emotions in between. Perhaps you have experienced something similar.

The truth I experienced was that external mosquitos were much easier to handle than internal ones. The advice to stay out of gossip and remain kind to your colleagues may carry you far in your organization. Internal mosquitos may require support from trusted friends, family, and professionals. A trusted friend does not need to be part of your organization. In fact, you may find that having someone outside of your work to talk to helps you maintain perspective and encourages you. Your family can be an immense support in a similar way—they love you but may not have a deep understanding of your day-to-day work, so they can discuss without the temptation to "talk shop."

Working with a professional counselor or therapist may make a significant difference as you receive bias-free support. A professional can help you do some honest self-reflection while simultaneously offering encouragement. Any form of support may be helpful, but not if it allows you to wallow and prevents you from taking steps to make things better! In my time working with a professional therapist, I found that I was able to swat away internal mosquitos and gain tools to prevent them from coming back.

Carla's Response

I experienced a devastating mosquito bite during an epidemic of encephalitis, which causes inflammation of the brain, and I became very ill. It was the summer I graduated from college with my bachelor's degree and got married. I was somewhat run down from working three jobs that final semester while taking a full load of classes and planning a big wedding. I went on a family picnic, and a mosquito got me! I had the worst headache of my life. I saw my physician, who provided me with medication to help me endure and recover from the illness. Nevertheless, it weakened my immune system and led to another serious illness. Mosquitoes, whether real or metaphorical, can cause a painful experience.

Like Sarah's colleague, I have experienced metaphorical mosquitoes at work. I was a leader among leaders in a very large organization, and I had just transferred to a new division and department. On most days, around lunchtime, I could hear noise permeating the thin wall between my office and that of my colleague next door. I recognized the voices to be the occupant of the office and a couple of our colleagues. The talk was loud, and so was the laughter. Not only was the noise distracting, but it was somewhat disturbing. I knew they were buzz talking about happenings at work and wondered if they might be laughing about me for reasons I could not imagine. It went on and on for some time and occurred frequently. They had a habit of going off to lunch together and never inviting me to join them. As Sarah said, this kind of mosquito bite hurts and then itches. I ruminated over why anyone would be so exclusive of me. I was definitely not "in" with them, and that made me itch.

My first thought was, "Who has time to play around like that during the workday?" I had more work to do than I could handle. My second thought was, "Why did they not invite me to join them for lunch?" I felt left out because I was, indeed, left out. Eventually, I shared with a trusted colleague and friend whose office was in another part of the building about the loud voices, guffawing, and exclusive lunches. I told my friend how I felt left out. Her immediate response was, "Do you want to be included in their playful talking sessions and lunches?" The question gave me pause. I realized I did not have time nor did I really want to be part of their hilarity. Like Sarah's friend, I decided to remain an outsider and keep my peace of mind. However, it hurts to be excluded. By anyone. Eventually, I developed relationships with each of these individual colleagues, and those relationships were based on work. When they were with me one-on-one, they did not buzz and behave in surprising and confusing ways. I realized they did not dislike me, but rather they knew somehow that I was not like them. I learned to let them buzz without me and away from me and not let them hurt me, make me itch, or interrupt my day.

That sounds easier than it is to do. Humans are social creatures, and we do not want to be left out. As a people person, I naturally want to be part of what is going on with the people I know in any setting. Making a conscious decision to not engage as a mosquito was unsettling at first. But the longer the clamorous behavior continued, the less I desired to be part of it. I knew I did not want to be a mosquito, but I did want to be part *of the team. It was difficult and even somewhat painful to be nearby and not included. As Sarah suggested, I sought the counsel of a true friend and of my husband. They gave me the encouragement I needed to stay out of it and maintain my professional demeanor.*

As I reflect on those days of being somewhat ostracized while also inflicting some level of isolation on myself, I realize a few leadership lessons. First, if you want the respect of others, then keep your professional demeanor, and do not become a mosquito. Second, remember that it is simply not nice to make fun of other people, so do not do that. Third, if you continue to treat the mosquitoes with respect and keep the conversation on point when you need to engage with them, they may eventually come to respect you. Related to this third leadership lesson is the fact that, in my case, each of the leaders ultimately came to me for help with professional initiatives and treated me with the kindness and respect I had been giving them. So, in the end, I did not have to behave like a mosquito just to be liked and included.

Take Time to Reflect

- Have you ever struggled with accepting your own success? What do you feel is the cause?

- Who are the external mosquitos in your organization? Have you seen damage done by gossip?

- **Challenge:** This challenge is two-fold. Think about the internal and external mosquitos in your professional life. Write out three steps you will take to quiet your inner mosquitos and reduce the impact of external ones in your organization.

- **Making Progress:** What do you need? Whose help do you need to get there?

_____

_____

_____

_____

_____

_____

_____

_____

_____

_____

_____

BE THE MANATEE

BE THE MANATEE

*Where there are trusting relationships,
there are happy workers who tend to
collaborate and be productive.*

THE SHARK

How do I avoid hurting others?

In one of my early days as a central office administrator in a large public school district, a friendly colleague warned me, "Beware of the sharks in this place. You will be eaten by the sharks, or you will become a shark and eat others." I did not like those choices. I decided right then and even stated to my colleague that I would neither be eaten nor eat others. I became a student of leadership, and I am proud to say I stayed true to that claim over many years.

According to the National Ocean Service, people are not part of the natural diet of sharks.[18] So, why do they attack humans? It seems they attack humans when they are confused or curious. I can draw a parallel to humans who behave like sharks at work. Many times, when colleagues attack each other, it is because they are confused. So, how do we prevent a human-shark attack? Logic says to not create confusion.

If we go into a situation with transparency, other humans tend not to go on the offensive. By transparency, I mean to be clear, honest, and open. Help people understand why you are saying and doing what you are saying and doing. If you know people are not going to appreciate the message you must deliver, it is good practice to provide the history of the change or condition. It is good to create as much understanding around a topic as possible and then deliver the point of information that is most likely to create distress.

Most of my work, as a leader in education, has involved leading people through change. The difficulty for a change leader is that the human reaction to the idea of change is typically resistance. Change causes feelings of threat, loss, and confusion. Some people call these feelings *disequilibrium*. And we know that confusion or disequilibrium in sharks is a reason for an attack. To help people through those difficult feelings related to change, leaders have to help them avoid an attack. According to Heifetz, Grashow, and Linskey, "Adaptive leadership almost always puts you in the business of assessing, managing, distributing, and providing contexts for losses that move people through those losses to a new place."[19] What is key in such leadership is "to be able to do two things: 1) manage yourself in that environment and 2) help people tolerate the discomfort they are experiencing. You need to live in the disequilibrium," (see Footnote 19). As a leader, it is important to understand the changes that are occurring in the organization, whether they are initiated by others or by you. When you understand the reasons behind the changes and the steps that will likely occur to make the changes, then you can manage your own feelings of disequilibrium, which is critical to being able to help others manage their feelings of disequilibrium.

I have found that telling the truth is a good way to keep predators away. If you build trust by consistently being honest, and even going beyond honesty by venturing into the practice of transparency, then potential predators often become allies. My practice of telling the truth has kept me from being a predator too. It is difficult to eat people, to cause them pain or harm, while being honest and transparent.

Being kind is another way to stave off predators. Good news, bad news, and neutral news can all be delivered with kindness. Avoid being a shark, and engage in random acts of kindness. Avoid creating confusion by being clear and kind. It is a good idea to seek out others in your organization who are kind and may save you from the sharks.

When I was an experienced teacher and serving in a teacher leader role, my principal was the opposite of a shark. He was quite brilliant, fun to be around, and fully aware of how his large faculty of over 100 people were feeling on any given topic, responsibility, or change. I recall one time when this principal asked me to accompany him to a training event on a big change the district was making. When I gave him a questioning look, he explained that I was going to be the person who would deliver the news to the very large faculty. I must have given him a shocked look at that point because he said he knew if he, as the principal, despite his kind nature, delivered the unwelcome news, the faculty would cry out with resistance. He went on to say that I was part of the faculty, the teachers liked and respected me, and they listened to me and followed my actions and even my attitudes. Wow! While I felt I had just received what my family calls "a big honking compliment," I also felt the weight of the burden my principal was asking me to carry.

I went with my very popular principal to the district-wide training event for administrators and soaked in as much information and understanding as I could that day. I knew a deep understanding, combined with a lot of self-reflection on the coming changes, would be critical to my delivery of information to the faculty. When the information sharing day came, the faculty gathered in the high school's auditorium, one of the few rooms on campus large enough to seat everyone. My principal called me to the microphone at the appointed time, and I began to share information with honesty and clarity. I openly admitted the negative side of the changes and what that might mean to the teachers, and I also shared what I, as their colleague, found to be the positive side and how I chose to frame the impending changes in my mind. I was consciously managing my own disequilibrium in front of the entire faculty so that they might do the same. I opened the floor for questions, and there were a few. I did my best to share details as clearly as possible. The meeting ended with no outcry or rebellion. A week later, I was promoted to a formal leadership position.

In the scenario I just described, my principal and I demonstrated adaptive leadership together. We were thoughtful and kind. Our approach helped the faculty face changes that were beyond their control with less fear and less sense of loss than they otherwise might have felt.

Perhaps another way to describe a kind leader is a resonant leader. According to Boyatzis and McKee,

> Leaders who can create resonance are people who either intuitively understand or have worked hard to develop emotional intelligence—namely the competencies of self-awareness, self-management, social clarity, not simply following a whim or an impulse…Emotionally intelligent leaders manage others' emotions and build strong, trusting relationships. (see Footnote 12)

My principal was a resonant leader. He inspired that quality in me. We were a good team.

The opposite of a resonant leader is a dissonant leader. These leaders "wreak havoc…They drive people too hard, for the wrong reasons, and in the wrong directions. They leave frustration, fear, and antagonism in their wake. And they are often completely unaware of the damage they have done," (see Footnote 12). The dissonant leader is a shark who leaves colleagues wounded or worse.

I once worked under the direction of a dissonant leader. She exemplified all the traits described by Boyatzis and McKee. After eight months, I found a new place to work. I left hurt, emotionally damaged, doubtful of my worth, and wondering how this had happened to me when I loved the work I was doing. Then I watched 100% of the people on that dissonant leader's staff leave during her first year of shark-style leadership. New people were hired into those half dozen positions, and in another year, they all fled too. While that level of attrition validated my feelings, it was a terrible blow to the organization. The shark seemed unfazed. As Boyatzis and McKee said, that shark was "unaware of the damage" she had done. Or, she did not care.

Additional anti-shark traits are empathy and compassion. Empathetic and compassionate behavior among humans can go a long way toward building trusting relationships. In my professional experience, where there are trusting relationships, there are happy workers who tend to collaborate and be productive. Honesty, transparency, kindness, empathy, and compassion are a winning combination of leadership traits.

Sarah's Response

I remember working for a really nice person early in my career. They were kind, supportive, and generally had the support of those they led. However, after a couple of years, an organizational change took place above this leader's head, and the fallout of the new, controversial policy rippled through the group of people they supervised, including myself. The staff was basically divided in half. Drawing parallels to a shark, there seemed to be some semblance of confusion on the leader's part as to how to move forward because they had caused a significant amount of disequilibrium by not clearly and kindly rebuilding unity. Individuals on the staff may not have experienced a personal "shark attack" from this leader, but as a member of the staff, it felt as though a proverbial shark attack took place on the morale and cohesiveness of the staff due to the leader's actions (or lack thereof).

The disequilibrium was perpetuated by the leader's inaction. Without words of encouragement or clarity in the face of the new and frustrating organizational policy, in-fighting took place, as some carried on with their work despite the change while others wanted to meet the change with protest. Friendships among staff members, which had lasted for years, ended. The awkwardness was palpable, and most days, I left

irritated, sad, and burdened, as my empathetic brain tends to hold others'
emotions and my own. Even harder still, there was no explanation for
the leader's inaction. Speculation may have suggested that their hands
were tied, and they were advised by their own supervisor to avoid taking
a stance on the new policy. Still, simply saying that much may have
subdued the emotionally charged atmosphere that lasted for months.

I wish there were a good ending to this story. The truth is, I'm not
sure how well the staff recovered because I left. A lot of people left. I did
not leave directly because of the environment created by the confused,
shark-like behavior we all experienced from our leader. I left for
unrelated personal reasons, but I can confidently say those reasons could
have been overcome, and I may have stayed if the environment had been
healthier.

There are commonalities between this chapter and the thoughts
Carla and I shared in the chapter about the gray wolf. The big takeaway
for me is that in order to retain a high-quality staff, leaders must act
with kindness, empathy, clarity, and direction. When that doesn't happen,
people leave. Good people. As you've read, Carla and I have both left
positions due to the behavior of leaders that was metaphorically aligned
with that of the shark or the wolf. I have many colleagues who have done
the same at some point in their careers.

I am not saying that leaders do not deserve empathy when facing
a difficult situation. I am sure that the situation to which I referred was
difficult for my leader at the time. As a leader myself, I encourage you to
seek guidance and support from mentors or colleagues when faced with a
particularly difficult situation to avoid your staff feeling the effects of a
moment of confusion or conflict. Change is hard, and there will be tough
situations ahead. But by avoiding the addition of prolonged pain when
change occurs, you can help your staff and team members navigate the
disequilibrium well and ensure they stay.

Take Time to Reflect

- Have you ever worked for a shark? How did it make you feel to work for a shark?

- Reflect on a time when your boss treated you with honesty, transparency, kindness, empathy, compassion, or any combination of these leadership qualities. How did that boss make you feel? What was the outcome of your work together?

- **Challenge:** Think about a time when you brought out the very best in another person—child or adult. How did you do it? What character traits did you exemplify? Think about the leadership traits you want to utilize when leading others.

- **Making Progress:** What do you need? Whose help do you need to get there?

_____

_____

_____

_____

_____

_____

_____

_____

_____

_____

BE THE MANATEE

BE THE MANATEE

*Workaholism can be an asset in
helping my productivity level, but
then it can be a liability too.*

THE HONEYBEE

How do I avoid becoming a workaholic?

Many animals may be considered workaholics. Among them are earthworms, shrews, wrasses, salmon, ants, Arctic terns, honeybees, beavers, lions, and rabbits. Honeybees, for example, work six ten-hour days to produce 2.5 mL of honey, while the queen bee lays more than 1,000 eggs a day. Beavers constantly work, building dams, canals, and lodges with the purpose of protecting themselves from fast-flowing water and predators. Ants are interesting. Notably, they spend most of their time gathering food and defending, cleaning, and tending to their young. [20]

Like these animals, I am a workaholic. Many leaders bear the burden of working many hours beyond the workday and working on weekends. Working six ten-hour days like the honeybee is not unusual in the world of leadership. Spending time tending to our young as the ants do is what educators live for! However, at times, the workaholic nature can become too much and can actually hurt others, as well as the workaholics.

Let the Work Begin

My workaholism began when I was a little girl in elementary school. I remained busy with schoolwork, dance lessons, baton twirling, Girl Scouts, piano lessons, handbell ringers, Sunday School, then eventually voice lessons, pep squad, sewing, interest clubs, a service club, flag twirling, church youth group, and all manner of school activities and events. My mom wanted me to "be involved" and experience many things. She was a child during the Great Depression and did not have the opportunities I had, and she worked to provide me with every opportunity possible. But at the same time, my mom knew when too much was just too much. She tried to get me to slow down, but I kept running.

When we keep running, eventually, we get run down and then sick. When I became ill as a teenager, my mother scolded me, "I told you if you did not slow down, your body would make you." That statement is emblazoned in my brain, as I heard it every time I got sick. Then, of course, my mom would compassionately care for me.

In college, I continued to be a workaholic. In fact, during my senior year, I carried a full load, worked three part-time jobs, and planned my wedding. It was overwhelming. As time moved on, I realized that workaholism does not just go away. It is a trait that is in the fiber of my being. It can be an asset in helping my productivity level, but it can also be a liability.

Three weeks after completing that hectic senior year of college, I married my sweetheart on June 24, 1978. During those three weeks between commencement and my wedding, I got a summer job. Then I landed a teaching position that started in August.

I was bitten by a mosquito that introduced me to encephalitis that same summer. I kept going while recovering from that serious illness. What I did not realize at the time was how severe encephalitis is. It can be deadly. It can also depress the immune system, which is what happened to me. While still recovering from encephalitis, I started that new and coveted teaching job and threw myself into it as my new husband and I settled into our new-to-us home.

By Christmastime, with my depressed immune system, I contracted what was then called viral hepatitis from eating seafood. I had no idea what I was in for. First, there were two weeks of complete bed rest. Two days after I was allowed out of bed, I relapsed, and my physician sent me right back to bed for another two weeks. During that time, I lost twenty pounds due to the side effects of the illness. When I was pronounced well, I was considerably underweight and lacked energy. One would think I had learned something about working too much, but no, I pressed on. It took ten years and two pregnancies to recover those twenty pounds and the robust feeling of being truly well and healthy. Finally, I slowed down—a little bit.

The Working Mom

Being a working mother is a typical lifestyle in America. Most mothers with full-time careers resemble ants. If you study an ant hill, it appears that the little ants are all running to and fro without ever stopping. They seem to continuously move the dirt of their anthill from here to there. They look to be in constant motion. That was how I behaved while teaching high school and raising two children. I had school activities, and they had school activities. I had homework (papers to grade), and they had homework. They had sports and dance lessons, and I had to take them to the events and cheer them on. Additionally, we had church activities on weekends, as well as meals with extended family. We were a lot like the ants in constant motion, and I was the organizer of all that motion.

When my children got a bit older, I wanted to become a National Board Certified Teacher by earning certification from the National Board for Professional Teaching Standards (NBPTS). To do so, I had to develop a daunting portfolio that demonstrated my teaching skills. It had to be completed between November and April (the time frame is now a bit longer since the

NBPTS moved to digital portfolios). This was when I first learned to delegate like the honeybee and not like the ant. I called a family meeting to discuss my desire to work toward National Board certification. My husband and both children thought it was a good idea.

I then shared that all my time when not at school teaching would have to be spent developing that portfolio and writing the extensive narrative it required. Therefore, I would need the three of them to take over my responsibilities at home and divvy up my chores. They all agreed. That experience of delegating my responsibilities to others, who had more time and were quite capable of doing them, was a great lesson for me on the importance of delegation. Because I sought their opinions and support and then had their cooperation, I finished the portfolio on time and passed the certification requirements.

I have discovered, as you may have as well, that our behavior at home and at work are often the same. The problem I have found with the delegation of work in schools and district offices is the inconsistency of having staff members available to support the leader's work. Nevertheless, it is important to find others who can take over some of the tasks we are doing that they can do just as well, so we can focus on leading.

> Successful teams share lots [in common] with a beehive. Everybody knows their role and can work independently. One tool to foster a more hive-like environment is delegation. So, if you want a hyper-productive team that can function without you, think of bees and hives...Create autonomy and empowerment to enable your team to work efficiently without a centralized leader.[21]

The point is to be more like the honeybee–delegate and collaborate–and less like the ant in constant motion with no apparent purposeful goal.

The Beehive Effect

As a district administrator in a large public school system, I had a mountain of responsibilities and minimal staff based on funding allocations. I had been encouraged by some high-performing teachers I respected to volunteer to host a national symposium. That would include: helping other leaders see the value in having this symposium in our city, acquiring funding, identifying and securing keynote speakers for each day of the event, recruiting experts in the field to facilitate breakout sessions, securing a facility, organizing the time frames and other details for each day of the symposium, marketing, and on and on. How would I manage all that with no other staff members and only the support of one secretary, whom I shared with another administrator? First, I recruited the teachers who were excited about this initiative in the first place. They became my guiding coalition.[22] I should pause here and explain that a guiding coalition is a group of effective people who help lead an initiative or change. We held planning sessions in the afternoons when they were free to leave their various schools and met in a central location to plan and execute the work. I also talked it up in the office. I found that not only was my shared secretary excited about this initiative, but other clerical staff in my department were willing and enthusiastic about getting involved in supporting the work. Even my family members enthusiastically joined in with the work involved in presenting the symposium. Instead of becoming exhausting drudgery, planning and implementing the national symposium became a fun and highly successful experience that impacted educators and leaders across the nation. Delegation and collaboration were the keys.

Sarah's Response

As I read about Carla's journey through school and into her professional experience, I see a lot of myself there too. I often found myself involved in many activities as a student and professional; I am always pushing myself, always reaching for that next step, and always getting involved in organizations. If someone asks me to be a part of something, nine times out of ten, the answer is an emphatic ,"Yes!"

I could not agree more that leadership requires delegation and collaboration. Even if we want to do everything, even if we have the knowledge and capacity to do everything, we will falter at some point from a lack of time, personal resources, or exhaustion. Leaders have a responsibility to empower others and trust their abilities. That empowerment is vital to the health of the organization. Bringing up new leaders can help you avoid being a workaholic and ensure that someone is there to take over if you are absent for a day, a week, or when it's time to retire.

There is a catch that I think is important to note. Collaboration, delegation, and distribution of tasks require you, the workaholic leader, to let go. This may be difficult for a workaholic because we like to do everything. We may also be convinced that the way we do something is better than the way other people do it.

Delegating may require practice for you, and that's okay. A good first step is to consider the task at hand. Are there a number of ways to accomplish the same thing that are equally effective? Also, consider the people you are entrusting the task to—does this play to their strengths? If there is a lack of skill or competency in the task, is this an area they are passionate about and want to grow in? If the answer to those questions is "yes," it's time to let go! As your team works through the project, resist the urge to check in all the time. If you are spending time hovering over the completion of a task you delegated, did you really delegate?

After the work is complete, evaluate how you feel. At first, you may struggle with a final product or presentation moving forward without your touch, without your approach. Listen to the feedback of your customers, clients, or colleagues. Chances are, everything went just fine, and that's great because it means you can continue to delegate to your team, knowing that there will be a good outcome. There are some projects that you will want to retain control over, which is appropriate if it is assigned to you specifically and your job role is imperative to completing the task. This advice is not carte blanche to never work again; it is permission to let go of the things that will grow the capacity of others, increase productivity, and encourage collaboration while simultaneously getting you out of the hive.

Take Time to Reflect

- Are you a workaholic? Do you take on tasks that others can do for you or with you? If so, why do you think you work this way?

- Consider a time you behaved like a workaholic and it hurt you and possibly others around you. How could you have handled things differently? How can you delegate and collaborate with a guiding coalition in the future?

- **Challenge:** Think about a time when you delegated some of your work to others who could do it and had more available time than you did. How did that turn out? What did you learn from that experience?

- **Making Progress:** What do you need? Whose help do you need to get there?

_____

_____

_____

_____

_____

_____

_____

_____

_____

_____

_____

_____

BE THE MANATEE

Epilogue

We sincerely hope you enjoyed reading about our leadership adventures, our successes and missteps, and the lessons we learned along the way. So, now what? As you reflect on your own practice as a leader, whether you are an informal leader to whom others naturally look for advice and guidance, or you are a formal leader with a title that gives you authority and the responsibilities that come with authority, you may want to consider a few final thoughts from us.

Consider how you will protect your peace. Find your helpers and get help if you need it. Build a guiding coalition or a support network. Build up your own competencies. Think about who you really are and how you want to handle yourself when you are surrounded by negativity. Consider what you will do in those discouraging moments when you feel useless. Plan ahead on what you will do to handle yourself through the inevitable challenges you will endure as a leader.

Reflect on your skillset for leading others. Consider what you will do when the people you lead think differently than you do. Think about the various ways in which others respond to leadership and what they need from you. If you are a new leader, determine ways you will help your team to work together harmoniously and be happy to have you as their leader.

Contemplate how you will avoid toxic behavior. Consider how you can avoid feeling intimidated. Plan how you will avoid hurting others. If you know you have workaholic tendencies, then give some thought as to how you can delegate appropriately and utilize your team effectively. Determine how you will handle situations when other leaders, or even team members, display destructive behavior.

It can be difficult to truly define what we are feeling or how to give a name to a situation we are in—that is why we chose to use animal metaphors. We hope you remember the capybara when you need to relate to someone who thinks differently than you or the honeybee when you feel overworked and overwhelmed. Our parting wish for you is that you find the strength and support you need to lead well, and if you hit a rough patch along the way, always remember to *be the manatee.*

Footnotes

1. Manatees 101. (n.d.). *Ocean Today*. https://oceantoday.noaa.gov/manatees101/welcome.html#:~:text=Manatees%20don't%20really%20have,species%20are%20endangered%20and%20threatened

2. McMahon, M. (2019). There's more to hibernation than you think. *Forest Preserve District Will County*. https://www.reconnectwithnature.org/news-events/big-features/more-to-hibernation-than-you-think

3. Di Silvestro, R. (2016, January 5). 10 things you may not know about groundhogs. *National Wildlife Federation Blog*. https://blog.nwf.org/2011/01/10-things-you-may-not-know-about-groundhogs/

4. Bat Echolocation. (n.d.). Maryland Department of Natural Resources. https://dnr.maryland.gov/wildlife/Pages/plants_wildlife/bats/batelocu.aspx

5. Gray, R. (2015, April). Eye knew it! Markings on butterflies really DO mimic a predator's gaze. *Mailonline*. https://www.dailymail.co.uk/sciencetech/article-3030780/Eye-knew-Markings-butterfly-wings-really-mimic-predator-s-gaze.html

6. Bowerbirds. (n.d.). Bush Heritage Australia. https://www.bushheritage.org.au/species/bowerbirds

7. Schultz, C. (2014, February 7). Capybaras are basically nature's chairs: The world's largest rodent can't get any respect. *Smithsonian Magazine*. https://www.smithsonianmag.com/smart-news/capybaras-are-basically-natures-chairs-180949677/

8.   Alex, A. (2022). 5 giant leadership traits we can learn from female elephants! *ActiveRain*. https://activerain.com/blogsview/5697216/5-giant-leadership-traits-we-can-learn-from-female-elephants-

9.   Robin. (2016). Elephant leadership. *Wamvenga Creative Coaching*. https://www.wamvenga.com/blog/post/elephant-leadership/

10. Sommer, T. (2018). Leadership animal #3: The elephant: Only healthy teams can consistently perform at a high level. *Rebubble*. https://medium.com/redbubble/leadership-animal-3-the-elephant-77a0f9f41489

11. Walraven, E. (2019). What wild animals can teach you about leadership. *Financial Review*. https://www.afr.com/work-and-careers/leaders/what-wild-animals-can-teach-you-about-leadership-20190902-p52n64

12. Boyatzis, R. & McKee, A. (2005). *Resonant leadership: Renewing yourself and connecting with others through mindfulness, hope, and compassion.* pp. 4, 6, 22. Harvard Business School Press.

13. Meyer, F. (2013, October). How octopuses and squids change color. *Ocean: Find Your Blue*. Smithsonian. https://ocean.si.edu/ocean-life/invertebrates/how-octopuses-and-squids-change-color

14. Greenwald, M. (2020, October 23). 25 adorable animals that mate for life: These birds, reptiles, and mammals are all monogamous. *BestLife*. https://bestlifeonline.com/animals-mate-for-life/

15. Animal Ark. (2021). Gray wolf, canis lupus. *Animal Ark Wildlife Sanctuary*. https://animalark.org/education/learn-about-animals/family-canidae/gray-wolf/

16. Mosquito bite symptoms and treatment. (n.d.). Centers for Disease Control and Prevention. https://www.cdc.gov/mosquitoes/mosquito-bites/symptoms.html#:~:text=When%20a%20mosquito%20bites%20you%2C%20it%20pierces%20the%20skin%20using,to%20a%20bite%20or%20bites.

17. Weir, K. (2022). Feeling like a fraud? American Psychological Association. https://www.apa.org/gradpsych/2013/11/fraud

18. National Ocean Service. (2021). Do sharks hunt people? *National Oceanic and Atmospheric Administration (NOAA)*, U. S. Department of Commerce. https://oceanservice.noaa.gov/facts/sharkseat.html

19. Heifetz, R., Grashow, A., & Linsky, M. (2009). *The practice of adaptive leadership: Tools and tactics for changing your organization and the world.* (pp. 22-23, 29). Harvard Business Press.

20. Oregon Farmers. (2017, August). Most busiest animals in the world. *Protect.* https://www.protectoregonfarmers.com/most-busiest-animals-in-the-world/

21. Sommer, T. (2018). Leadership animal #2: The bee. *Redbubble.* https://medium.com/redbubble/leadership-animal-2-the-bee-cbc79f45adde.

22. Kotter, J. P. (2012). *Leading change.* Harvard Business Review Press.

Acknowledgments

We would like to acknowledge our colleagues who provided support throughout the process of writing our book. Thank you, Dr. Christie McMullen, Dr. Lorrie Butler, Dr. Stefanie Shames, Dr. Daniel Buckman, Dr. Rosita Riley, and Dr. Bradley Fuller. Whether you provided feedback, guidance, encouragement, or a combination of all three, we would not have finished this without you. We are both so lucky to call you our friends.

We would like to acknowledge the team at Two Penny Publishing for their partnership and helping us accomplish this goal.

Sarah would also like to acknowledge Daniel Lukas, Tanya and Fred Turner, Margaret Mayhew, Holly Turner, Dr. Sarah Tierney, Dr. Jesus Castro, and Melissa and Adrian Kunkel. Thank you for always being there and for being a constant source of encouragement. You are amazing people, and I am truly lucky to have you in my life.

Carla would also like to acknowledge Vance Sparks, Katie Sparks Jones, Wes Sparks, Vincent Jones, Vera Sparks, and Estelle Sparks Jones. Thank you for always, always believing in me. Thank you for giving me the time and space to do the work I love. I knew I could do this because you knew I could.

A special thank you to Katie Sparks Jones for sharing her artistic talent with us and providing the illustrations of our animals.

Dr. Sarah Lukas   Dr. Carla Sparks

About the Authors

Dr. Sarah Lukas

After several years of teaching middle school social studies, Dr. Sarah Lukas began serving in leadership roles, including an instructional coach and school district administrator. Sarah earned her doctorate in 2020 from National Louis University where she was lucky enough to be paired with Dr. Carla Sparks for her dissertation chair. She currently serves as a school administrator in a large public school district and an adjunct professor for National Louis University. Her educational and professional interests include leadership development, scholarly writing, and reading instruction. Sarah lives in Florida with her husband, Daniel.

Dr. Carla Sparks

Dr. Carla Sparks spent more than 30 years in K-12 public education, the last 10 years of which she served as a district administrator in one of the largest public school districts in America. Carla is a "double alum" of National Louis University where she earned her Master of Education degree in Curriculum and Instruction and her Doctor of Education degree in Educational Leadership. She currently serves as the Faculty Lead for Educational Leadership Programs at the Florida Regional Center of National Louis University. Her professional interests are in change leadership, project-based learning, graduation by exhibition of mastery, and differentiated instructional practices. Carla lives in Florida with her husband Vance, adult children, and grandchildren.

Made in the USA
Monee, IL
26 April 2023

32540468R00103